VIKINGS

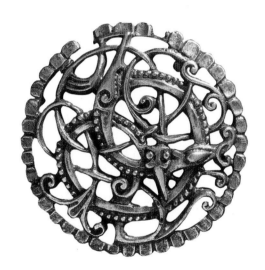

VIKINGS

THE BATTLE AT THE END OF TIME

TONY ALLAN

DUNCAN BAIRD PUBLISHERS

LONDON

HALF-TITLE PAGE An 11th-century bronze brooch known as the Pitney Brooch after the village in Somerset, England, where it was found.

FRONTISPIECE A detail from the wooden cart dating from the first half of the 9th century that was found with the Oseberg ship near Oslo Fjord.

VIKINGS

First published in the United Kingdom and Ireland in 2002 by
Duncan Baird Publishers Ltd
Sixth Floor
Castle House
75–76 Wells Street
London W1T 3QH

Managing Editor: *Christopher Westhorp*
Editor: *James Hodgson*
Designer: *Paul Reid at Cobalt id*
Picture Researcher: *Cecilia Weston-Baker*
Commissioned artworks, decorative borders and map: *Peter Visscher*

Editorial Consultant: *Hilda Ellis Davidson*

A CIP record for this book is available from the British Library

Hardback: 10 9 8 7 6 5 4 3 2 1   Paperback: 10 9 8 7 6 5 4 3 2 1
Hardback ISBN: 1-903296-56-0   Paperback ISBN: 1-903296-62-5

Typeset in Perpetua and Bernhard Modern
Colour reproduction by Colourscan, Singapore
Printed and bound in Singapore by Imago

NOTE
The abbreviations BCE and CE are used throughout this book:
BCE Before the Common Era (the equivalent of BC)
CE Common Era (the equivalent of AD)

CONTENTS

IMAGE AND IMAGINATION

LEFT **An elaborately crafted ship's prow symbolizes the Viking tradition of seafaring. The prow comes from a replica of the Oseberg ship, excavated in 1904 from a 9th-century burial mound that contained the bodies of two women—probably a queen and her attendant.**

BELOW A taste for intricate decoration was as much a part of the Norse people's mindset as a love of the sea. This filigree brooch comes from a group of graves excavated in the 1880s in the Vendel district north of Stockholm.

In little over 250 years, from the late eighth to the mid-eleventh century, the Vikings transformed Europe. Starting as raiders, they became in time explorers, conquerors, lawmakers, and founders of nations. In Iceland they created northern Europe's earliest republic; around 2,000 miles (3,200 km) to the south-east they laid the foundations of the Russian state. Norwegian settlers founded Ireland's first cities, while in far-off Constantinople, Swedes provided the Byzantine emperor with his personal bodyguard.

Above all, though, the Vikings were seafarers. Norse mariners, carried in longboats, traveled farther north and west than any previous European peoples, establishing a colony on the west coast of Greenland and beating Christopher Columbus to America by almost 500 years.

THE SOUL OF THE VIKINGS

In the year 793 CE, news of an unimaginable atrocity spread through Christian Europe. Ship-borne raiders from across the North Sea had descended upon Holy Island (Lindisfarne), off the coast of northern England. The rich treasures of its famous monastery had been plundered, its monks killed or dragged off to slavery. In a savage age, Europe's monastic foundations had long been seen as havens of culture and learning. Now it seemed they were no longer sacrosanct.

The Holy Island cataclysm was one of the first Viking assaults, but it was quickly followed by others. In the ensuing years, similar hit-and-run raids devastated ecclesiastical communities on the coasts not just of England but of Scotland and Ireland too. Before long, towns were also being targeted, and within just 60 years of the first sorties, boat-borne invaders were threatening whole kingdoms.

It is hard to exaggerate the impact that the Viking raids would have had on the rest of Europe. They came at a point when firm government, in the hands of rulers like Offa (died 796) in the English kingdom of Mercia, and Charlemagne (ca. 742–814) on the Continent, had been restoring order after the troubled centuries following the collapse of the Roman Empire. And they fell upon some of western Christendom's holiest sites, refuges of peace and learning in a strife-torn world.

To their horrified contemporaries the pagan Vikings seemed embodiments of terror and destruction, sent by a righteous God to punish a wicked world. That image was slow to fade, not least because most of the written sources describing their activities were the work of Christian churchmen.

In recent times, though, that negative portrayal has been reappraised. A series of stunning archaeological finds has emphasized the Norsemen's positive achievements as traders, travelers, craftsmen, explorers, settlers, and finally rulers. Increasingly they are now seen not just as a destructive force but as a vitally creative

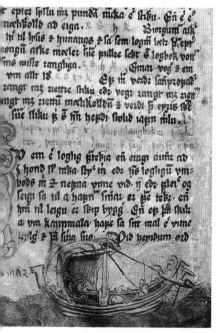

A miniature painting of a boat at sea decorates the margins of a 16th-century copy of the *Jonsbok*, the Icelandic legal code. For nearly two centuries before they were first set down in writing, the Viking republic's laws were transmitted orally, recited aloud annually before the national assembly.

one. Ferocious they undoubtedly were, but their relentless determination and dauntless courage acted as catalysts for change in an otherwise stagnant world. As well as fire and the sword, they brought ambition, enterprise, and boundless energy to peoples whose horizons were for the most part limited, rarely stretching beyond the bounds of the nearest village.

Even though most of the Norse men and women of the Viking Age were content to stay at home and work the land like their southern neighbors, the scent of adventure and excitement clings stubbornly to the Viking name. They may have been relatively few, but those youths—many of them younger sons in want of an inheritance—who went out in search of wealth and glory were the agents of historical change. With limitless audacity they set out to take on the world, and in so doing they altered it indelibly.

The ruins of a medieval Benedictine priory mark the spot where Viking raiders descended on the monastic community on Holy Island, off England's Northumbrian coast, in 793. The raid is often taken as the starting point of the Viking Age.

THE STORY OF THE VIKINGS

The term "viking" started off as a vocation, not a group name. Restless spirits chose to "go viking," which meant raiding. They came from the Norse lands that would one day be known as Denmark, Norway, and Sweden, but at the start of the Viking Age they did not think of themselves as Danes, Norwegians, or Swedes. At the time their loyalties were altogether more local, tied to a neighborhood or else to an individual warchief. The concept of nationhood only came later; it was in fact one of the achievements of the Viking Age.

Although the Norse peoples often fought among themselves, they nonetheless had much in common. They shared a language (Old Norse) and a religion—the worship of Odin, Thor, and the other northern gods. They came from roughly similar societies, divided broadly among three classes: a warrior nobility; a wide category of freemen, including in its ranks merchants, craftsmen, and especially the *bondi*, or landowning farmers; and thralls, or slaves. Good agricultural land being a limited resource, there was always, both among the *bondi* and the nobility, a restless subclass of younger sons with no estate to inherit; it was from their ranks above all that the Viking raiders were recruited.

Although the northern lands were little known to other Europeans at the time, the Norsemen themselves inherited a footloose tradition. They were the natural successors of the Germanic peoples who had fanned out across Europe during the Age of Migrations from the second century CE on, among them the so-called "barbarians" who helped bring down the Roman Empire in the fifth century.

The Norsemen also inherited a tradition of trading dating back to the Bronze Age (ca. 2000–500 BCE), when fur and beads of Baltic amber—fossilized conifer resin—were already sought-after luxury goods over much of Europe. Even so,

This 9th-century bronze amulet depicting a horned figure holding a sword and two spears was found in a grave in eastern Sweden. It may represent a cult leader sacrificing to the god Odin.

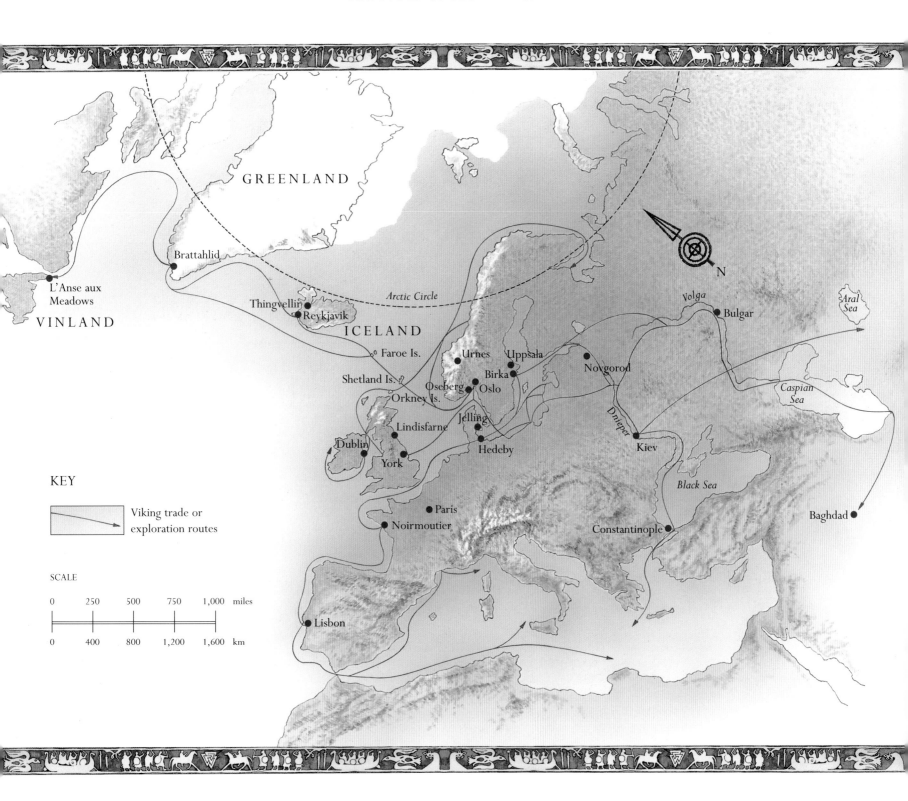

GREENLAND

L'Anse aux
Meadows

VINLAND

Brattahlid

Thingvellir

Reykjavik

Arctic Circle

ICELAND

Faroe Is.

Urnes

Uppsala

Birka

Volga

Bulgar

*Aral
Sea*

Shetland Is.

Oseberg

Oslo

Novgorod

Orkney Is.

*Caspian
Sea*

Lindisfarne

Jelling

Dnieper

Dublin

York

Hedeby

Kiev

Black Sea

Paris

Noirmoutier

Constantinople

Baghdad

Lisbon

N

KEY

Viking trade or
exploration routes

SCALE

0	250	500	750	1,000	miles

0	400	800	1,200	1,600	km

A silver pendant made in south-eastern Sweden around the year 1000 represents a moustachioed warrior wearing a helmet with a nose-guard. It may have been worn on a neckchain as a lucky charm for protection in battle.

Scandinavia remained something of a backwater until the Viking irruption. Historians still argue over the underlying causes that suddenly drove so many Norsemen far beyond their own shores. Technological improvements in shipbuilding played a part in making the exodus possible, but they could not in themselves provide a motive. Population pressures were undoubtedly a factor, but they seem not to have been dramatically worse than in previous ages; estimates suggest that there were never more than two million people in all the Scandinavian lands throughout the Viking era. Indeed, conditions actually seem to have been improving at the time; a slight but significant warming of the climate caused glaciers to recede, made winters more endurable, and may have lessened infant mortality, creating a greater number of landless younger sons to go adventuring.

The first to venture abroad in significant numbers were the Swedes, whom geography directed eastward. Their main thrust was across the Baltic Sea and into Russia down the great river systems. Taking over an existing Slav settlement at Novgorod in the late ninth century, they turned it into a key trading post controlling two major routes to the south. One followed the Dnieper down to Kiev, where a second center was established, and then on to the Black Sea, opening the way to the Byzantine capital of Constantinople. The other took boat-borne travelers almost 2,500 miles (4,000 km) down the Volga to the Caspian, beyond which caravan routes led on to Baghdad.

The lure that drew the traders southward was silver, particularly coins from the mines of Arabia. In return they traded furs—sable, squirrel, beaver—and slaves, many of them taken as booty or tribute from the Slavic peoples among whom they traded: the very word "slave" derives from "Slav." Trading elided all too easily into raiding, and Viking warriors launched assaults on mighty Constantinople itself, in

860 and again in 907. Although both were repulsed, the second came close enough to success to persuade the Byzantine emperor to come to terms, offering trading rights to the Norsemen in return for guarantees of peace as well as the provision of bodyguards—the famous Varangian guards—for the emperor's own person.

The Viking impact on Russia was even more marked, for the settlers—known to the Slavs as Rus, from a Finnish word meaning "Swede"—played a vital part in setting up the first organized Slavic state. As the *Russian Primary Chronicle* (ca. 1112) tells the tale, the Rus were approached by the leaders of warring tribes, who told them: "Our land is great and rich, but there is no order in it. Come to

An illustration from an 11th-century chronicle shows the Byzantine emperor Theophilus making a proclamation flanked by the Varangian Guard (see pp.82–3). The Varangians were Norse mercenaries chosen for their fighting skills to serve as the emperor's bodyguards.

Ruined fortifications originally built to repel Viking raiders stand guard on the River Ulla in the region of Galicia in north-western Spain. From 844 on, ship-borne Norse warriors launched a series of attacks on Spain's Atlantic coast and on into the Mediterranean beyond.

reign over us." The Rus took them at their word, setting up a joint Swedish–Slav state that came to bear their own name, first at Novgorod and later at Kiev.

While the Swedes looked east, the peoples of Denmark cast their eyes to the south; their influence was most keenly felt in England and in the lands of Charlemagne's Frankish Empire, which at the time included not just France but Germany and the Low Countries as well. At first the empire's strength provided a bulwark against attack, but when in 840 it split between three rival heirs, the Norsemen seized their opportunity. On Easter Day in 845, Vikings attacked Paris after venturing 100 miles (160 km) up the River Seine.

From the 850s on, the Danes' tactics changed. Instead of simply staging short, hit-and-run raids, they started overwintering in the lands they raided, operating from semi-permanent bases at the mouths of rivers. The next logical step was full-scale occupation, and in 865 the first of many mighty Danish armies arrived in England. At the time the country was divided between a half dozen rival kingdoms, most of which were not strong enough to repel the invaders. East Anglia soon fell, and others quickly followed, until by 880 only the southern realm of Wessex held out. There an outstanding ruler, Alfred the Great, stemmed the tide, but by that time the Danes had already established their hold over more than half of England. In the area under their control, the Danelaw, they left a permanent mark, bequeathing to succeeding generations the concepts of a written law and of trial by jury. They also made a lasting contribution to the English language: such everyday words as "take," "die," "sky," "anger," "hell," and "ugly" all have Old Norse roots.

The Danelaw in turn provided a base for further raids on France, until in 911 King Charles III decided to buy off the raiders by offering their leader, Rollo, lands around the mouth of the Seine in return for a promise to fight off rival Vikings. Rollo kept his side of the bargain, and before many generations had passed, his Norsemen transmuted into Normans, accepting the language and the Christian religion of their subjects. It was Rollo's sixth-generation successor Duke William of Normandy who in 1066 successfully invaded England, bringing the entire nation under Norman control.

While the Danes were conquering kingdoms, the Norwegian Vikings were exploring less charted areas of the globe. Most of their raiding centered on Scotland and particularly Ireland, where they established coastal settlements that developed into the island's first towns: Dublin, Wexford, Waterford, and Limerick are all Norse foundations. They also settled on offshore islands, including the Isle of Man, the Orkneys, and the Shetlands. They provided the Faroe archipelago, almost 450 miles (700 km) west of Norway, with its first permanent residents; previously the islands had served as a summer retreat for Irish monks.

Carved gables and a boat design decorate a house at Hedeby, an important Viking trading center in southern Denmark. A modern reconstruction built using traditional methods, the house now forms part of an open-air museum on the site.

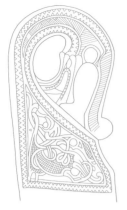

According to tradition, in about 860, two separate crews, one bound for the Hebrides and the other for the Faroes, were blown off course and discovered a previously unknown island. News spread, and within the decade settlers began to arrive to take advantage of the new land's empty acres. Over the next century Iceland developed as an independent realm with the most democratic system of government yet seen in northern Europe, dominated not by a single ruler but by 36 local patriarchs, each the spokesman for his own district, who met annually in an open-air assembly known as the Althing (see p.108). By the late tenth century the island had 60,000 inhabitants—almost a quarter of the population of Norway at the time.

Once all the good pasturage in Iceland had been claimed, adventurous spirits had to look further afield for virgin territory. A late tenth-century outlaw named Eirik the Red, sentenced for murder in both Norway and Iceland, sailed 450 miles (725 km) to the west in search of a fresh land whose existence had been rumored for many years. To encourage settlers, he gave the forbidding landmass that he eventually discovered the appealing name of Greenland. The stratagem worked; by the 980s a colony of several hundred immigrants was established there, living by farming, and hunting whales and walrus.

One would-be settler, leaving after the rest of the fleet, lost his way en route and came within sight of a shoreline of low hills that lay too far to the south to be the destination he sought. When he eventually reached Greenland, his story encouraged Eirik the Red's son, Leif Eiriksson, to venture further west in search of the

LEFT **Named a UNESCO World Heritage Site in 1978, the settlement at L'Anse aux Meadows on the coast of Newfoundland has been reconstructed to show how it might have looked when Vikings stayed there around the year 1000.**

RIGHT **Sunshine breaks through cloud around the islet of Stora Dimun in the Faroes group. Norse colonists were the first permanent settlers of the islands, set midway between Norway and Iceland in the North Atlantic (see p.85).**

mystery land. The result was probably the first European landfall in the Americas, made in 1001, when Leif arrived first at Baffin Island and then at L'Anse aux Meadows near Newfoundland's northernmost tip. Leif's achievement was a fitting climax to an extraordinary saga of exploration and adventure that within little more than two centuries had seen the Norsemen radiate out from their Scandinavian homeland to Baghdad and beyond in the east and to the New World in the west, conquering kingdoms and founding states and cities in the lands in between.

RAIDERS OF THE FJORDS

The fjords of western Norway not only served as bases for some of the earliest Viking raiders; they may also have given them their name. The derivation of the term "Viking" is usually traced to the Old Norse *vik*, meaning "inlet" or "bay." The original Vikings, in this interpretation, were seafarers who lurked in their boats in any of the many steep-sided sounds that gouge Norway's deeply indented North Sea coast, waiting to pounce on the cargoes of ships traveling

the North Way—the maritime trade route up to the White Sea from which Norway possibly took its name. These wily coastal pirates were not short of hiding-places; the littoral twists and turns along 15,000 miles (25,000 km) of deeply serrated shore, even though it stretches for less than a tenth of that distance as the crow flies. For this reason journeys along the Atlantic-facing coastline of Norway were expressed in terms of time not distance—a tendency that has continued into the modern era.

THE ART OF THE VIKINGS

BELOW Viking craftsmen often employed their talents to magnificently decorate relatively mundane objects. This gilded representation of an animal's head adorned one end of a wooden horse collar, used to pull a wagon in 10th-century Jutland.

The Viking way of life, with many individuals crammed into smoky, earth-floored dwellings, would hardly seem to have encouraged the accumulation of art objects. In fact, the Norse peoples had a passion for display that encouraged their craftsmen to transform everyday utensils into objects of beauty. The strength of their craving is reflected in myth in the story of Freyja, goddess of love, and her lust for the marvelous necklace known as the Brisingamen; its makers, four dwarf master-craftsmen, would only agree to give it to her if she slept with each one of them, an offer she unhesitatingly accepted.

Apart from poetry, all Viking creativity was expressed in what would now be called the decorative arts. People used the wealth that flooded into Scandinavia from raiding and trading to buy beautiful yet practical everyday objects, not art for art's sake. The creators themselves were almost always anonymous craftsmen, typically in the employ of kings or chieftains; only at the end of the period did individual artificers add their names to some rune-stones, and then mostly in a single area of central Sweden.

Much of the work must have been done in wood and textiles, but few examples of these survive. Stone carving is also poorly represented, at least for the earlier period; although there was a long-standing tradition of stonework on the Baltic island of Gotland, the taste

RIGHT This buckle clasp from Åker, in Hedmark, Norway dates from the 7th century. Made out of gold, silver, and precious stones, it vividly demonstrates the wealth that trade had already brought to the northern lands even before the start of the Viking Age proper.

only developed elsewhere from the mid-tenth century on, perhaps in response to a growing familiarity with Christian monuments from other parts of Europe. There is also little in the way of pottery; Vikings evidently preferred to eat and drink from unbreakable wood or soapstone vessels.

What has survived in the greatest quantities is metalwork, of which there was a longstanding craft tradition in Scandinavia. As early as the second millennium BCE, Norse artisans were among the finest bronzeworkers in Europe, even though they had to import much of the tin and copper needed to make the alloy. Among their masterpieces were the twisting ceremonial horns known as lurs, which curled up like convolvuluses as far as five feet (1.5 m) above the player's lips.

By Viking times, the metalworkers' wares were put to innumerable uses. They included brooches and ornamental pins used to fasten the thick woolen cloaks worn by both men and women; necklaces, armbands, and bracelets; charms and amulets; caskets for storing valuables, sometimes with inset panels of carved walrus ivory; horse collars and harness decorations; windvanes to ornament the prows of longships; and of course splendidly embellished weapons.

Viking taste demanded decoration that was vigorous, striking, and above all intricate, with much interlacing and interweaving. Throughout the period, the principal motifs were taken from nature. The starting point was most often an animal, though the beasts in question were frequently stylized almost to the point of

LEFT This silver cup, bearing traces of gilt and the blacking compound known as niello, comes from a burial mound at Jelling in Denmark (see p.30) that was constructed to house the body of Gorm the Old, father of the Danish ruler Harald Bluetooth.

RIGHT The Mammen style of Viking art took its name from the site in Jutland where this ornamental axhead was found. Made of iron inlaid with silver, the weapon was buried about the year 970 alongside the body of a nobleman from Harald Bluetooth's court.

abstraction; plants also started to appear regularly from the mid-tenth century onward. Representations of people were comparatively rare, and when they did appear they were usually (although not always) treated in a semi-naturalistic way that contrasted with the liberties taken with the bodies of birds and beasts.

Art historians trace six stages in the development of Viking art, marked by subtle changes in the style of decoration employed; the evolution of taste seems to have been dictated by master-craftsmen responding to art objects from overseas. The earliest style, exemplified by bridle mounts found in a grave at Broa on Gotland, was the first in Scandinavia to employ a specific motif known as the "gripping beast"—this involved an animal, often placed at the head of the design, whose paws enclose the other elements. The next two periods, known as the Borre and Jellinge, were largely contemporaneous, both flourishing from the mid-ninth to the late tenth centuries. Both feature so-called "ribbon creatures," whose bodies interlace in serpentine patterns; Borre pieces also sometimes employ a ringchain motif that is of a type employed today on metal watchstraps. Good examples of the Borre style come from the celebrated Gokstad ship burial.

In the mid-tenth century, the Jellinge designs developed into the Mammen style, which takes its name from the decorations on an axhead found at Mammen in Jutland (see p.23). The animals are more substantial in these works, though quite as fantastic in the contortions of their writhing bodies; in addition, plant motifs begin to show through in the form of shoots and looping tendrils. Such masterpieces as the Bamberg casket and the serpent-entwined beast on Harald Bluetooth's memorial stone at Jelling fall into this category.

Plant motifs became even more important in the ensuing Ringerike period, which succeeded Mammen at the turn of the eleventh century; by this time foliate patterning had become a regular feature. This tendency reached new heights in the Urnes period, the final phase of Viking art, which takes its name from a church at Urnes in Norway. The intricate design of interlaced animals, stalks, and tendrils on the eleventh-century wooden paneling on the church's walls (see pp.38–9) recalls the work of the arts-and-crafts designers of nineteenth-century Britain.

For all the elaborations, it is the consistency of taste throughout the Viking Age that remains most striking. The great change was to come at the end of the era with the adoption of Christianity, which opened the floodgates to foreign influence. By the twelfth century, newly converted Scandinavia had embraced the Romanesque style of the lands to the south and was well on the way to joining the mainstream of European art and design.

LEFT The head of a mythical beast adorns one end of a wooden horse collar found at Søllested on the Danish island of Fyn. The entire collar was richly decorated with ornaments in the Jellinge style, distinguished by delicately interlaced patterns of sinuous animals.

RIGHT Wood was probably one of the materials most favored by Viking craftsmen, although relatively little of their work has survived. This panel—one of a series illustrating the Sigurd legend—decorated a church doorway at Hylestad in Norway.

SECRETS OF THE RUNES

For most literate peoples the power implicit in the written word has been so long taken for granted that it now fails to excite wonder; but for the Vikings the runic alphabet always retained traces of primeval magic. Its origins are still shrouded in mystery, although it was shared with other Germanic peoples and was in use for many centuries before the Viking Age.

For the Vikings, one of the great advantages of runes was that the letters consisted entirely of straight lines that could easily be chiseled. People who lacked paper and pens could still notch a runic sentence on a stick of wood – probably the normal writing medium. However, most of the 4,000 or more inscriptions that survive are in stone, metal, or bone—many are gravestones, giving the name and sometimes also personal details of the deceased; others were used as road markers, or else served to identify the owners of weapons or caskets.

Yet there was also a more magical aspect to runes, little of which now remains as a result of the coming of Christianity and the ensuing destruction of all things pagan. The Viking peoples themselves explained the characters' origins by harking back to myth. Legend told that it was Odin himself who first acquired the mastery of writing, and he did so by undergoing a terrible ordeal in which some mythographers see parallels with Christ's crucifixion. To obtain the secret, Odin voluntarily underwent what might now be termed a near-death experience, hanging on Yggdrasil, the great ash tree linking the three worlds of the Viking cosmos (see p.38), and gashing his side with a spear. This enigmatic

Runic characters cover a stone found at Røk in the Swedish province of Östergötland. Set up by a father in memory of his dead son, it contains the lengthiest surviving runic inscription, made up in all of more than 700 symbols.

incident survives only from a single ancient source, a poem called the *Hávamál* ("Words of the High One") preserved in the *Poetic Edda*:

I know that I hung / On the windswept tree / For nine whole nights /

Pierced by the spear / And given to Odin / Myself to myself /

On that tree / Whose roots / Nobody knows / /

They gave me no bread / Nor drink from the horn / I peered into the depths /

I grasped the runes / Screaming I grasped them / And then fell back.

The implication would seem to be that runes came from the dark domain of Hel, Queen of the Dead, in Niflheim far below the worlds of gods and men, and with them Odin also seems to have acquired the mastery of occult wisdom—the very word "rune" derives from the Old Norse *run*, or "mystery." Although few clues now remain, it seems likely that runes played an essential part in the ritual sacrifices of the Viking era—for which they had to be reddened with blood to be effective—and they were also used to cast lots for divination.

Their role in the working of charms and spells is better attested. Some Viking amulets bear runic messages that apparently increased their magical potency, while one of a ring of standing stones at Björketorp in Sweden carries an inscription that speaks of "runes of might" and invokes a curse on anyone destroying the megaliths.

There are also clear implications in literature of the magical role that runes played in daily life. In the Icelandic sagas they are used to help in childbirth, to bring health or sickness, to make warriors victorious, to calm storms, and even to make the dead speak. One particular tale, recounted in the thirteenth-century *Egil's Saga*, describes how the hero traced the cause of a girl's sudden illness to a rune-inscribed whalebone hidden in her bed. Learning that she had an unsuccessful suitor, he charged the young man with witchcraft, only to learn that he had meant no harm; although the suitor had indeed carved the runes as a would-be love-charm, he was a novice at the art and had made a simple mistake in the writing. The saga drew the wise conclusion: *Let no man carve runes to cast a spell / Unless he first learns to write them well.*

Oddly demonic in appearance, this horned mask decorates a runestone found at Århus in Denmark. An inscription on top of the stone indicates that it was raised by a blacksmith named Toke for a certain Troels, son of Gudemund, who "gave him gold and salvation."

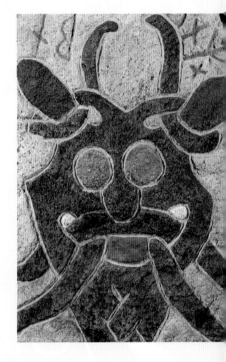

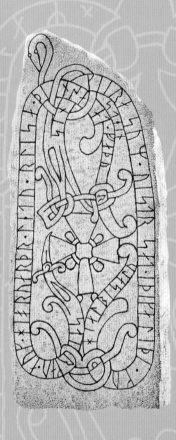

THE FUTHARK

To modern scholars the runic alphabet is known as the futhark, from the phonetic sounds attributed to its first six characters: f, u, th, a, r, and k. There were several different versions of the alphabet, of which the Scandinavian (seen in the inscription, opposite, from the smaller Jelling stone, see p.30) was the shortest, with just 16 characters. Each symbol served, in the manner of Egyptian hieroglyphs, both to represent a phonetic sound and also as a pictogram depicting an object or abstract notion. The first symbol of the alphabet, for example, not only stood for the letter "f" but could also mean "cattle" or "wealth." The limited number of characters in the Viking futhark caused some problems in that certain sounds were either not represented at all or had to double up. There were no separate symbols, for example, for the consonants "d," "g," or "p"— "t," "k," and "b" were used instead. The resulting ambiguities make some inscriptions difficult to translate.

KING GORM

: k   u   r m R : k   u   n   u k R :

MADE THIS MONUMENT

: k   a   r thi : k   u   b   l : thu   s i :

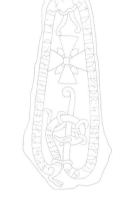

IN MEMORY OF HIS WIFE THYRI

: a   f   t : thu r   u   i : k   u   n u :

DENMARK'S ADORNMENT

: s i   n   a : t   a   n   m   a   r k   a R : b   u t :

RUNESTONES OF THE KINGS

The two royal runestones that stand side by side at Jelling in central Jutland are more than just magnificent monuments in their own right. Between them they mark a turning-point, not only in Scandinavian history but in that of Europe as a whole.

The smaller of the two was erected by Gorm the Old (died 958), founder of the dynasty that, under Svein Forkbeard and Knut the Great, would one day conquer England and rule a North Sea empire larger than any other of the Viking Age. Gorm set up the monument as a memorial to his wife Thyri (see pp.28–9); after his own death, the couple were buried together in a huge earth mound to the north of the stone.

The second, larger stone was also a memorial, this one to both Gorm and Thyri, and it was the work of their son Harald Bluetooth. Harald himself was a conqueror who temporarily brought parts of Norway under Denmark's sway; but he is now better remembered as the king who converted the Danes to Christianity, a feat commemorated in the stone's runic inscription. As well as the stone, Harald ordered the construction of a second barrow to the south of the site and also of a church—the first to be built in Denmark.

Three sides of Harald's great cenotaph are decorated. One bears a runic inscription commemorating his parents and listing his own achievements; a second bears a stylized image of the Crucifixion that is Denmark's earliest known representation of Christ. The image on the third side (shown here) harks back to traditional Viking iconography; it shows a dragon entwined by a sinuous serpent, a masterpiece of the Mammen style of Viking art (see p.24).

SAGAS OF GODS AND GIANTS

᛬ᚱᚨᛁᚦᚢᛚᚠ᛬ᛚᚨᚢᚠᚼᛁᚱᛒᛁᚱᚼ᛬ᛚᚨᚢᚠᛚᛁᛒᛁᚱᚾ᛬ᚱᚨᚦᚢᛚᚠ᛬

LEFT An enigmatic scene, possibly involving the gods Odin (wielding a spear) and Thor, decorates a 10th-century memorial stone, dedicated to two brothers from Sanda on the Baltic island of Gotland.

The Norse peoples venerated gods in their own image. Stories were passed down over farmstead fires and in kings' great halls of a pantheon dominated by deities who were first and foremost warriors: Odin the all-seeing schemer, a model of the cunning battle-leader; mighty, uncomplicated Thor, the fighter par excellence, unmatched in strength and courage. Yet there was also another, less familiar tradition of fertility goddesses and wise women, as well as tales of strange earth spirits—of giants, elves, trolls, and dwarfs. Hanging over all was a dark fatalism, for at the last the whole world of gods and men was to be swept away in a final apocalyptic encounter, the confrontation between the forces of good and evil the Vikings called Ragnarok.

BELOW Carved out of precious amber, this Danish gaming piece is thought to represent the god Freyr. Norse mythology is unusual in having two separate divine families, the Aesir and the Vanir, of which Freyr was probably the best-known representative.

THE VIKING COSMOS

Norse mythology paints an unusually clear picture both of how the world began and of how it will end. The vision of the beginning of things may have been influenced by conditions in Iceland, for it features a very Icelandic combination of ice and fire.

The world, as the myths tell it, grew out of a gigantic chasm: Ginnungagap, the Yawning Void. Ginnungagap was bordered to the south by Muspell, the abode of fire, where Surt the fire giant stood guard with a flaming sword. To the north lay the freezing land of Niflheim, later to be the land of the dead. Here 12 rivers bubbled up from a volcanic cauldron called Hvergelmir, pouring their waters into Ginnungagap. In its unplumbed depths they froze, gradually filling the mighty chasm. As the ice rose, it was touched by the heat of Muspell, and from the meeting came moisture that somehow transmuted into clay.

Eventually the clay took on life in the massive form of Ymir, the primeval frost giant. To provide Ymir with sustenance, another creature also took shape—a huge cow called Audhumla, the Nourisher, whose udder gushed forth milk. To feed herself, Audhumla could only lick the salty rime, and as she did so the outlines of a man began to appear under her probing tongue. This was Buri—the Producer—and he was to be the grandfather of Odin, greatest of the Norse gods.

By now the processes of creation were proliferating, for Ymir himself produced from his own sweat a couple who were to be the first of the giants, the gods' inexorable enemies; as the representatives respectively of good and evil, the two races were fated to irreconcilable conflict. Yet they could also fraternize from time to time—Odin himself was the result of a liaison between Buri's son Bor and a giantess.

Despite his mixed parentage, Odin grew up to be a scourge of the giant race, combining with his two brothers to destroy Ymir, whose blood gushed out in such a

RIGHT **Steam rises from a vent at Namafjall in Iceland. Norse creation myths imagined life as originating from the joint action of fire and ice— a peculiarly Icelandic combination that may have been suggested by the geysers and volcanoes that dot the island republic.**

flood that it drowned all his gigantic progeny, save for a single couple. These sur-
vivors fled to Jotunheim—literally Giants' Home—where they begot a new race
dedicated to the extirpation of Odin and all his kin.

With this work of destruction done, Odin and his brothers next turned to creation. From Ymir's body they fashioned the world as we now know it; his blood
became the seas and rivers, his flesh the land, his bones the mountains, and his skull
the sky. Four strong dwarfs, North, South, East, and West, were set to support the

corners of the firmament, while the
gods scattered sparks from Muspell
across it as stars. The sun and moon
were placed in chariots to follow each
other unceasingly across the sky, pursued by two fearsome wolves, Skoll
("Repulsion") and Hati ("Hatred"), who
at the end of time were fated finally to
devour the heavenly lights.

This "hogback" tomb at
Haysham in Lancashire,
England, may depict a pair
of dwarfs holding up the
sky. The tombs take their
name from their curved
profile, mimicking the
bowed shape of large
houses of the Viking era. An
alternative interpretation is
that the design represents
Christian figures raising
their hands in prayer.

Having fashioned the physical world, Odin and his brothers next created beings
to inhabit it. First came the dwarfs, who grew from maggots infesting Ymir's rotting
corpse; the gods gave them consciousness, and put them underground to search for
gold. In some myths these dwarfs seem to be confounded with the Dark Elves, similarly conceived as miners dwelling in darkness; in contrast, their radiant counter-
parts the Light Elves dwelled in the airy realm of Alfheim, near the gods' own halls.

After the dwarfs the three gods fashioned people—out of flotsam found on the
seashore. They assigned to the human race a central region, Midgard, ringed round
for protection with a fence made from Ymir's eyebrows. Only after Midgard was
made did they build their own home of Asgard, filling it with great halls and palaces.

Asgard could only be reached across a bridge guarded by Heimdall, the divine watchman. The bridge was called Bifrost, and to humans it appeared as the rainbow.

The geography of the Norse cosmos was never exact, varying in its details between different myths. Yet it was consistent in reflecting a multiplicity of worlds. Traditionally, there were nine in all, including those of humans, giants, and more than one race of gods; the lowest of all was ruled by Hel, dark goddess of the underworld, who was half living woman and half rotting corpse. The nine worlds coexisted uneasily; sometimes their respective inhabitants formed alliances, but at other times they plotted and fought against one another. And in this respect too the cosmos reflected the real world the Vikings knew: an uneasy place of shifting allegiances and competing realms, fraught with peril and ruled by an unforgiving fate.

Nearly 2 ft (0.6 m) long, the Trundholm chariot dates back to the Bronze Age. Its imagery suggests that the belief in the sun being drawn by horses across the sky may have predated the Vikings by 2,000 years.

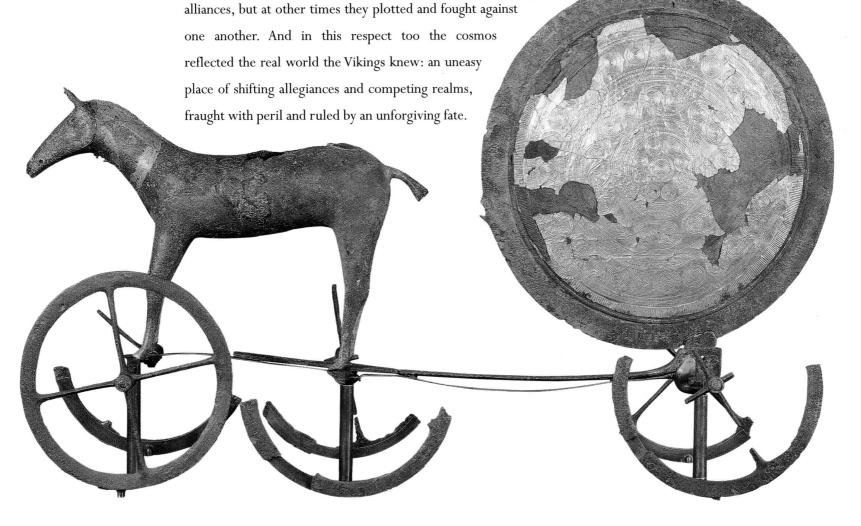

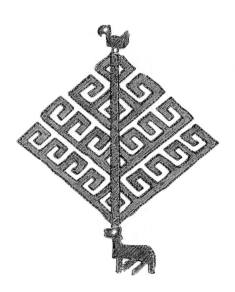

THE WORLD TREE

The great ash tree known as Yggdrasil—depicted symbolically in the wooden
panels of the church at Urnes, Norway (above)—was the pillar around which all the
various Norse worlds revolved. It rose through the middle of Asgard, and the gods
regularly assembled around it. It was said to have three main roots. One stretched
down to Niflheim and Hvergelmir, the seething cauldron in which life had
originated. Another grew in Midgard, where it was nourished by the Well of
Knowledge guarded by the wise giant Mimir. The third root sprang in Asgard. As
a living entity Yggdrasil was always at risk of decay; four deer fed on the tree,
nibbling its leaves, while the serpent Nidhogg gnawed tirelessly at its lowest root.
Constantly under threat but endlessly renewed, Yggdrasil was a symbol of life itself,
and its influence has endured. Maypoles and Christmas trees both possibly hark
back to it, while the notion inherent in it of a global axis survives linguistically in
the concept of a North and South Pole.

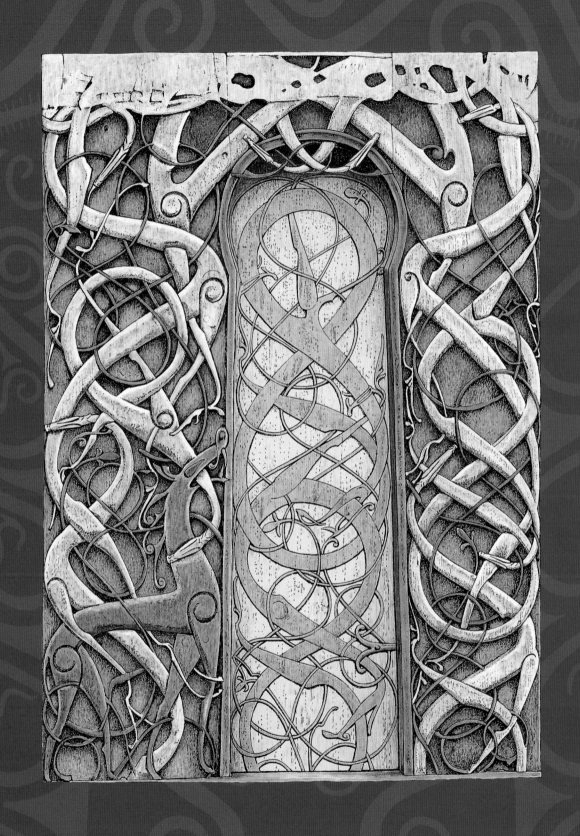

AESIR AND VANIR

The Norse world had not one but two divine families, no doubt originally reflecting different regional traditions. The larger and dominant group was the Aesir—the word means "gods"—who dwelled in Asgard and whose leader was Odin. Other important members of the group included Thor, Baldur, Heimdall, and the war god Tyr, and the goddesses Frigg, Sif, Nanna, and Iduna. In Odin and Thor, it provided two of the three most venerated deities of the old religion.

The third, Freyr, was the best known of the Vanir, the second group, along with his twin sister Freyja and his father Njord. Although in Viking times the Vanir were worshiped throughout the Norse world, their cult may have originated in Sweden. Certainly they seem to have been associated particularly closely with the Svear people from the central region of the country, and they came to be seen as the mythical progenitors of the Swedish royal house.

While Thor and Odin were warriors, Freyr and the Vanir were primarily linked with agricultural and sexual fertility. Freyr himself was represented ithyphallically with a prominent male member; Freyja was not only the goddess of love but, according to some myths, was also promiscuous. The Vanir's own fecundity extended to the fruits of the earth; they presided over sunshine, rain, crops, and all growing things, and their special season was spring, when Freyr was honored by ritual feasts and processions.

In the myths, the relationship between the two families was initially hostile. The first war was fought between the Aesir and the Vanir, and it was sparked, for reasons that the myths never make quite clear, by the Aesir's treatment of a giantess named Gullveig—the name means "love of gold." Three times they tried to kill her, by stabbing and burning, but on each occasion she survived. The Vanir rallied to her defense, and the ensuing hostilities eventually ended in

This bronze figurine from Lindby in south-eastern Sweden depicts a one-eyed figure probably intended to be Odin, chief of the Aesir family of gods, who sacrificed an eye in return for the gift of knowledge.

Three figures from a 12th-century tapestry that once hung in a Swedish church may represent leading Norse gods: Odin and Thor (left and center) of the Aesir, and Freyr (right) of the Vanir, holding an ear of corn.

a truce in which both sides exchanged hostages: Njord, Freyr, and Freyja went to live with the Aesir, while Honir and the wise Mimir joined the Vanir.

The most likely explanation of this enigmatic confrontation is that it represented in mythical form the accommodation reached between two rival sets of beliefs. Gullveig's punishment may represent symbolically the distaste felt by followers of the martial Aesir for the emphasis on wealth and prosperity in the Vanir's worship. If so, the aversion was successfully overcome, for subsequently both families coexisted as peacefully in myth as their respective votaries apparently did in the real world for much of the Viking Age.

ODIN, LORD OF SACRIFICES

Odin was not only the supreme Viking deity, he was also by far the most complex and enigmatic figure in the Norse pantheon. Known as "Allfather" for his part in the creation of humankind, he was also literally the father of several of the other Aesir, including Baldur and, according to some, Thor. Where Thor had his hammer, Odin bore the magical spear Gungnir, fashioned by dwarfs to hit its target without fail. He also possessed the finest of horses, the eight-legged Sleipnir, and was accompanied by a pair of ravens, Huginn and Muninn—literally Thought and Memory—which scouted the Norse cosmos, reporting back on what they saw.

In fact little escaped Odin himself, for from his seat high up on the rock of Hlidskjalf he could look out over the nine worlds of creation, observing all that happened in them. In search of more detailed information he would wander through Midgard in disguise, appearing to humans as a tall gray-bearded man in a long cape and broad-brimmed hat.

For all his deep awareness, though, he was a god who was respected and feared by his devotees rather than loved. For Odin, knowledge was power, and in the myths he went to extraordinary lengths to attain it. He was one-eyed, having sacrificed the other to obtain a draft from the Well of Knowledge. The god of poetry, he obtained the mead of poetic inspiration by taking on serpent form to worm his way, in the most literal sense, into the cellar where it was kept hidden by a covetous giant; then, in trickster fashion, he seduced the giant's daughter who guarded it in order to drain the barrels dry.

Most puzzling of all was the ordeal he endured to obtain the secret of runes (see pp.26–7). As the *Hávamál* tells the story, he hung on Yggdrasil for nine nights, wounded with a spear and "given to Odin, myself to myself," before he was able to snatch his prize. The meaning seems to be that he voluntarily made himself a

RIGHT **An unlikely figure for a supreme god, Odin was not just one-eyed but was also usually depicted as an old man. In this late-medieval representation, he is shown in the cape he wore to go wandering in the mortal world, armed with a sword and spear.**

A detail from one of the Gotland picture stones shows Odin on Sleipnir, his famous eight-legged horse. The small female figure shown greeting him may be one of his battle-maidens, the Valkyries.

sacrifice, just as prisoners of war and others were offered up to him in order to obtain a boon, which in this case was the secret of esoteric knowledge. The length of his ordeal may also have been significant, for the number nine seems to have had special significance in Odin's cult. The eleventh-century chronicler Adam of Bremen reported that the principal ceremony at the great temple of Uppsala in Sweden where Odin was worshiped was held once every nine years and lasted for nine days; in its course nine victims of every available species, including humans, were killed.

People apparently accepted such bloodthirsty rites because Odin was thought to bring success, above all in war. If Thor was the archetypal Viking warrior, Odin was nonetheless regarded as the principal god of battle, the "Father of Victories." As such, he was the patron of the aristocratic warrior class as a whole and of the royal houses in Denmark and Norway in particular. He was also the inspiration for the berserkers, followers of Odin who deliberately cultivated battle frenzy as a way of terrorizing opponents; his very name, meaning "raging" or "intoxicated," suggests the qualities they sought to display. It was Odin too who owned Valhalla, the Hall of the Slain, where the fighting dead were taken from the battlefield.

There are indications, mainly derived from the evidence of place-names, that Odin's cult was a relatively late arrival north of the Baltic, radiating upward from northern Germany and the Jutland peninsula not long before the beginning of the Viking Age. It seems to have been particularly weak in south-west Norway, where most of the settlers of the Atlantic islands had their origins. Perhaps for that reason, as well as for its royal connections, the cult appears never to have become firmly established in Iceland, which did not have a royal family; there Odin was invoked as the muse of poetry but does not seem to have been presented with offerings or sacrifices.

Yet even when he was not directly worshiped, the spirit of Odin haunted the Norse world. In the myths he was a pervasive presence, turning up repeatedly as a *deus ex machina* intervening unexpectedly but decisively in human affairs. He was at best an unreliable ally, who would grant a warrior victory one day only to abandon him the next. Sinister and all-seeing, he was a force that the ambitious courted, for no god had greater power, yet no one could count on his goodwill for long. Changeable in his moods and inscrutable in his actions, he was the embodiment of fate for the anxious human actors in an unpredictable, often violent world.

A pair of gilt and bronze harness mounts found on Gotland may represent Odin's two ravens, Huginn ("Thought") and Muninn ("Memory"). The birds were the god's spies, reporting back everything of interest that they saw on their daily flights around the world.

SPIRITS OF THE FORESTS

While wood was a scarce commodity in some parts of the Viking world—notably in Iceland and Greenland, where settlers had to rely on driftwood washed up on the beaches for most of their needs—other areas, including Denmark and central Sweden, were heavily forested. In these regions, trees quickly took on an enduringly numinous aura for the local population. As early as the first century CE, the Roman historian Tacitus wrote of the northern Germanic peoples worshiping their gods in forests, while a

millennium later the chronicler Adam of Bremen reported, in his description of the pagan temple at Uppsala, that the bodies of humans and animals sacrificed to the gods were left to hang in a sacred grove (see p.95). The association between trees and supernatural presences proved to be deep-rooted—well into the Middle Ages, a Norwegian law aimed at removing relics of paganism forbade people from believing that the forests were inhabited by earth spirits.

FREYJA, MISTRESS OF LOVE

Freyja was the goddess not just of love but also of birth, death, and fertility—the entire human cycle. One of the Vanir, she came to Asgard with her father Njord and her twin brother Freyr as part of the settlement following the war with the Aesir. She was associated with luxury and the love of beautiful things, and was not always scrupulous about how she obtained them; she consented to sleep with four dwarfs to win the priceless Brisingamen necklace. Yet she was also courageous—she alone was prepared to serve mead to the drunken giant Hrungnir when he threatened to destroy Asgard—and her anger could be fearful to see.

As the embodiment of sexual desire, she was noted for her lascivious, passionate nature. She was accused by Loki of having slept with all the Aesir including her own brother, while the giantess Hyndla charged her with chasing males like a nanny-goat in heat. In turn she incited lust in beings of all kinds: the giant Thrym stole Thor's hammer, planning to exchange it for Freyja, while the dwarf Alviss engaged in what turned out to be a fatal wisdom contest with Odin in the hope of winning her as his reward. Another myth told how the giant who built Asgard's fortifications demanded as payment the sun, the moon, and Freyja—a trinity that has been taken to symbolize all the forces of light, life, and growth.

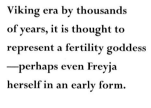

ABOVE Just 2.5 in (6.5 cm) high, this Bronze Age female figurine was found in Jutland. Predating the Viking era by thousands of years, it is thought to represent a fertility goddess —perhaps even Freyja herself in an early form.

BELOW Shown in semi-abstract form, Freyja wears the Brisingamen necklace in this Viking Age pendant, now on display in Stockholm's State Historical Museum.

The sun sets over a meadow by the Lyngenfjord in the far north of Norway. As a fertility goddess, Freyja was associated with flowers and all growing things, but also with human love; the chronicler Snorri Sturluson reported that "love songs are pleasing to her."

Freyja was a popular goddess, and her cult was widespread. Sometimes she was viewed as an emblem not just of passion but also of compassion—a Madonna figure as well as a Venus. "Goddess Beautiful in Tears," she was said to weep drops of gold for the waywardness of her wandering husband Odur, a little-known figure in the Norse pantheon who is sometimes thought to be Odin himself under another name. As the patron of procreation, she was invoked not just by lovers eager to further their cause but also by women in childbirth and in naming ceremonies for newborn infants.

Yet there was also a harsher side to Freyja's nature. Sometimes she haunted battlefields, sharing half of the kill with Odin and welcoming the warriors she chose to her hall of Folkvanger. And, again like Odin, she practiced magic—the powerful witchcraft known as *seid*. "The most renowned of the goddesses," as the *Prose Edda* calls her, she was a figure of power as well as of beauty, passionate by nature and steely minded in the extreme when it came to getting her way.

THE DIVINE THUNDERER

The strongest of the gods, Thor was also the most admired. A huge, red-bearded figure with flaming eyes and a fearsome temper, he seemed the very archetype of the brave Viking warrior. Celebrated for his giant-killing exploits, he was revered as the chief defender of Asgard and Midgard and as the protector of order against the forces of chaos.

The son of Odin and Jord ("Earth"), he lived with his wife Sif in a 540-room mansion, the biggest ever built. He traveled in a chariot drawn by two goats, Tooth-gnasher and Tooth-gritter, that had magical properties—they could be killed and eaten if food ran short, but so long as the bones were left intact they could be restored to life. Thor's other remarkable possessions were his hammer Mjollnir (see p.52) and a belt that had the magical property of increasing his strength by half whenever he wore it.

In the myths Thor features principally as the dedicated enemy of giants; several recount his feats of strength while out looking for trouble in Jotunheim. He killed the mighty Geirrod, for example, by catching a lump of molten iron that the giant threw at him and hurling it back with such force that it passed not just through Geirrod himself but also through the pillar behind which he was hiding, and then on through the building's outer wall. Yet his relations with the giant race were not always hostile. He even had two sons by a giantess, Jarnsaxa of the Iron Knife, and it was foretold that they would survive Ragnarok (see pp.62–5) and inherit the hammer Mjollnir in the new age that was to follow.

In the real world Thor was associated with the elements, and above all with storms; thunder was said to be the noise his chariot made as it careered across the

Thor clutches his hammer Mjollnir in this 10th-century bronze talisman from Iceland. The marked cruciform shape of the hammer may have been influenced by Christian imagery, which was beginning to gain a foothold at the time.

sky. Travelers invoked his protection whenever they set out on journeys, and every time that lightning flashed people remembered his power.

Perhaps as a result of his adoption by travelers, Thor's cult embraced the entire Norse world. On the evidence of place and personal names, he was the most popular of the gods; no less than 25 percent of the entire population of Iceland in Viking times had names featuring the word "Thor." He presided over the Althing, Iceland's annual assembly (see p.108), which opened on his day, Thursday; there and elsewhere in Scandinavia, oaths were sworn over his ring. In the temple at Uppsala his statue was said to hold the central position, between those of Odin and Freyr, and when a Christian missionary attempted to destroy the image he paid for his temerity with his life. Odin may have been the god of the northern aristocracy, but for the bulk of the population—farmers, craftsmen and the like—Thor reigned supreme as a powerful champion, a figure to turn to for help whenever danger threatened.

The valley in southern Iceland known as Thorsmork—literally, Thor's Forest—is one of hundreds of sites across the Norse world to bear the god's name. According to early sources, Thorsmork was named by its first settler, who hoped to gain divine protection by dedicating it to Thor.

THE HAMMER OF THOR

Thor's hammer Mjollnir was one of six treasures made for the gods by dwarfs, the master-craftsmen of the Norse world. The others included Odin's unerring spear Gungnir and his self-reproducing ring Draupnir; and, as gifts for Freyr, a boar with a golden mane and bristles, and a marvelous ship that could sail over both land and sea and could also fold up to the size of a pocket handkerchief. However, the Aesir judged the hammer the greatest of all the gifts for its value as a matchless weapon against their foes—not only did it shatter whatever it struck but it also magically flew back to Thor's hand whenever he threw it. For his human votaries, the hammer became popular in miniaturized form as a good-luck charm. Amulets made in its image seem to have been associated in people's minds with Thor's role as god of storms; in the myths Mjollnir sometimes seems to be confounded with the thunderbolts the god was imagined to throw, while some scholars have traced the name itself back to the Russian word *molnija*, meaning "lightning."

LOKI, MASTER OF MISCHIEF

L oki was a complex figure, a trickster who by the time of the final conflict of Ragnarok (see pp.62–5) had transmuted into a symbol of pure evil.

There were different versions of Loki's origins. The most probable make him the son of a giant; he only gained entry to Asgard by winning Odin's friendship— the two became blood-brothers. Quick-witted and handsome, he was also malicious and wily; Snorri Sturluson, the major source for the Norse myths, calls him "the slander-bearer of the Aesir, the promoter of deceit."

Some of the tales told about Loki follow a familiar trickster model in which an individual who is too clever for his own good gets a deserved comeuppance. So, having lost a bet that could have cost him his head, he once ended up with his lips sewn together—a fitting fate for a smooth talker. However, at other times his quick wits saved the Aesir from disaster. When a giant demanded the sun, the moon, and Freyja in payment for building a wall around Asgard, for example, it was Loki who prevented him from completing the task on time and so from claiming his reward.

Loki's stratagem on that occasion was to turn himself into a mare in order to distract the horse that carried the giant's supplies. The incident illustrates his magical powers of shape-shifting—and in this case also of changing sex. The story also displays his role in the myths as a begetter of monstrous progeny, for from the union of the stallion and the mare Odin's eight-legged steed Sleipnir was born. Others of Loki's offspring were altogether more sinister in their powers; the giantess Angrboda bore him a fearsome brood consisting of Hel, Queen of the Dead, the World Serpent Jormungand (see p.61), and the ravening wolf Fenrir.

Jormungand and Fenrir were both fated to play a decisive part in Ragnarok, as was Loki himself. In this final incarnation, he revealed his true nature once and for all: malice personified, breaking all the bonds of order to bring chaos again.

RIGHT This figure on a furnace stone from a forge at Shaptun in Denmark may be Loki depicted with his lips sewn together. He earned the punishment by losing a bet as to which of two dwarf master-craftsmen could produce the finer work.

GIANTS, DWARFS, AND MONSTERS

The Viking cosmos was crowded. Humans lived there alongside not just two separate families of gods but also giants, elves, and dwarfs. Although the giants were defined in Norse myth by their role as the gods' adversaries and eventual destroyers, relations between the two races were far from exclusively hostile. There were, in fact, many stories of liaisons between gods and giantesses. Thor himself was born of the union between Odin and Jord, while Freyr and Freyja were the offspring of the marriage between the Vanir god Njord and the giantess Skadi. Giants could even on occasion show kindness, as they did to the young prince Agnar, rightful heir to a kingdom that had been usurped by his brother; making his way to Jotunheim, Agnar found shelter and fair treatment of a kind that had eluded him in the human world.

Generally, though, the giants were depicted in the myths as dull and slow-witted—Loki regularly outfoxed them. Giants were fearsome above all for their huge size, for they towered even over the gods—in one comic tale, Thor and Loki mistook a giant's discarded glove for a building, spending the night in one of its fingers.

As creatures of the cold and the dark, giants could not stand the sun, turning to stone if its rays fell upon them. They shared that characteristic with dwarfs, who lived underground where sunlight never shone. The dwarfs were renowned as master-craftsmen—responsible for fashioning such marvels as Thor's hammer Mjollnir in their subterranean workshops. The trolls, too, made their homes under-

RIGHT The mythic world of the Norse peoples was multi-layered. Many of the beings that populated it, including giants, trolls, dwarfs, and Dark Elves, were thought to live in cavernous subterranean realms.

LEFT An unlikely decoration for a baptismal font, this 12th-century carving from Gotland shows a dwarf—one of the skilled metalworkers of Norse myth—busily employed at his forge.

ground, although the mounds in which they lived had tops that could be raised on pillars to let in daylight. Savage and uncouth, the trolls resided in Jotunheim alongside the giants, often acting as their servants.

The elves were altogether more complex in their derivation. They had some ritual significance, for householders offered sacrifices to them at the start of winter, apparently as a fertility rite. Their profile was ambivalent in the extreme; the Light Elves were considered almost as beautiful as the gods, while the Dark Elves were misshapen and hideous. Memories of both traditions survived into the folklore of later ages, respectively in the form of the fairies and the goblins.

SERPENTS AND DRAGONS

Snakes are not common in Scandinavia, so the frequent occurrence of serpents in the myths probably owes more to worldwide patterns of storytelling than to everyday familiarity. Although they had their own mythic role, snakes were often confounded with dragons, not least in real life; the longboats of Viking raiders were known as *drakar*—dragon ships—but the mightiest of them all, constructed in the year 998 for King Olaf Tryggvason of Norway, was called the Long Serpent.

In Norse myth, snakes have almost entirely negative connotations. Living in burrows, they were associated with the underworld and hence with the dead. Their poison was dreaded—Loki's punishment for the slaying of Baldur was to lie bound while snake venom dripped onto his face. The greatest threat to the World Tree came not just from the serpent Nidhogg but also from many other snakes that attacked its roots; the ancient poems name a half dozen of them.

The role of dragons was altogether more complex. They inspired fear, as snakes did, but on a much grander scale; their fiery breath could burn up a shield in a twinkling, and their scales were impenetrable to sword thrusts, so that only their soft underbellies were vulnerable to attack. Again like snakes, they lived underground, in their case in the Bronze Age burial mounds, often the size of small hills, that dotted the northern landscape. Because of their subterranean habits they could only emerge from their lairs after sunset—a poet refers to one as "the old night-flier."

Dragons had a very specific role in Germanic and Scandinavian mythology as the guardians of buried treasure—a reflection of the very real hoards of precious grave-goods that often lay in the tumuli they were imagined to inhabit. Sometimes

LEFT **A dragon's head adorns the top of an elaborately carved wooden post, one of five that were found among the grave goods in the Oseberg ship burial.**

RIGHT **Sigurd slays the dragon Fafnir in a detail from the carved doorposts of Hylestad church, Norway. According to the legend, the hero hid in a trench so that he could stab upward into the creature's unprotected underbelly.**

in the literature they seem almost like the lust for gold made incarnate. In the Sigurd saga, for example, Fafnir, having killed his father to obtain possession of the dwarf Andvari's cursed treasure, physically transmutes into a dragon to watch constantly over it. Yet however repulsive they seemed, dragons were also repositories of esoteric knowledge. Fafnir was reputedly infinitely wise and had advance knowledge of what would happen at Ragnarok, while by accidentally tasting the dragon's blood Sigurd acquired the ability to understand the language of birds.

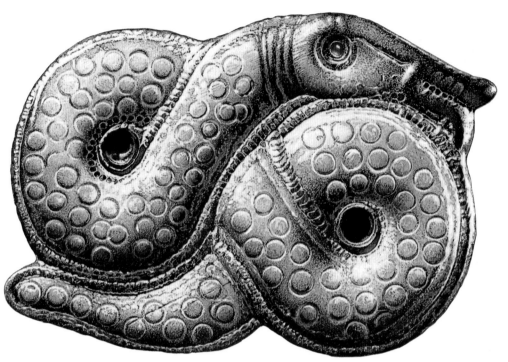

THE WORLD SERPENT

By far the most terrifying of all the snakes of Norse myth was Jormungand, the World Serpent. One of three monstrous children born to Loki and the giantess Angrboda, it was cast into the sea by Odin, who foresaw the great harm that the creature would do at Ragnarok (see pp.62–5). There it grew until its body encircled the earth, biting on its own tail. In one story a giant challenged Thor to lift a cat off the ground, yet try as he might Thor only managed to raise one of its paws. Only after the event did the giant confess that the cat was in reality none other than Jormungand; seeing its paw move, the giant had panicked, fearing that Thor might indeed raise it from the depths, bringing disaster on the world. In another tale, Thor went fishing for the World Serpent with a different giant, baiting his hook with the head of the giant's prize ox. Again he came close to success, dragging the serpent up to the water's surface. However, before he could kill it with his hammer his companion cut the line, letting the monster sink back into the waves.

THE BATTLE AT THE END OF TIME

The account given of the end of the world in Norse mythology is unique; no other tradition, except perhaps that of the biblical Book of Revelation, has such a detailed vision of how the final catastrophe will occur. The story is told allusively in two poems, in each case put in the mouth of an individual with access to hidden knowledge; in the *Völuspá* (ca. 1000), the longer of the two, the speaker is a female seer described as being cunning in magic.

The story of Ragnarok, the Doom of the Gods, had a profound effect on the Norse worldview, contributing greatly to its mood of fatalism. It told how, ultimately, the worlds of gods and men would be swept away. Even Odin and Thor, the mightiest of Asgard's defenders, could do no more than delay the onset of the final battle, in which they must inevitably meet their own deaths.

This silver figurine was found at Birka, in Viking times a leading Baltic trading center. The horseman may represent a warrior-king or else a hero riding to Valhalla.

The prelude to Ragnarok is the death of Baldur, son of Odin and Frigg and the best-loved of all the Aesir. Having heard that her son is destined to be killed unwittingly by another of Odin's sons, the blind Hod, Frigg asks all things animate and inanimate to swear not to harm him. However, Loki, now become a figure of pure evil, discovers that Frigg had forgotten to ask the mistletoe. He hands a branch of mistletoe to Hod and directs the blind god's aim toward Baldur—the mistletoe pierces Baldur and he dies. When Frigg goes to the underworld realm of Hel, Queen of the Dead, to request his resuscitation, it is Loki again who thwarts her mission. In retaliation, Loki is bound with the entrails of his own son Narfi and left pinioned on three sharp rocks to await the day when Ragnarok shall dawn.

As Snorri and the poets tell the story, its coming will be heralded by a time of savage warfare among men—"an ax age, a sword age, a wind age, a wolf age." Then there will be a terrible winter lasting for three whole years. The wolves that have

RIGHT A matrix used to produce decorative metal plaques shows a man with a bound animal—perhaps the god Tyr with Fenrir, the monstrous wolf he chained at the cost of his own hand. The matrix dates from ca. 700 CE.

long pursued the sun and the moon will finally catch and devour their prey; the earth itself will quake and trees and crags will be uprooted.

Three cockerels will crow, one on the gallows tree, one in Hel, and one in Valhalla, to signal that the forces of evil have finally been unleashed. The wolf Fenrir will break its fetters, and Jormungand, the World Serpent, will rise up from the sea, scattering venom from its mouth. All the Aesir's enemies will gather for battle. Surt will lead the fire giants from Muspell; as they approach Asgard, the rainbow bridge Bifrost will buckle under their weight. Stirred up by Jormungand, the ocean will flood into Hel, tearing the ship Naglfar from its moorings; this terrible vessel is made of nail-clippings taken from the dead (humans can delay its completion by sending corpses to the grave with their fingers and toes trimmed). Loki will burst free from his bonds to pilot it toward Asgard, accompanied by Hrimir and the frost giants and all the champions of Hel.

Meanwhile in Asgard, Heimdall, the divine watchman, will blow his horn to signal the alarm. The World Tree will tremble, and giants and dwarfs alike will quake

A fragment from northern Iceland, thought once to have formed part of an 11th-century Doomsday from Hólar cathedral, shows a beast swallowing a human figure. For the island's surviving pagans, the image would no doubt have recalled the wolf Fenrir swallowing Odin in the showdown at Ragnarok.

In a detail from one of the picture stones found on the Swedish island of Gotland, of which nearly 400 have survived, a dead human warrior (according to one interpretation of the source) rides to Valhalla, to be welcomed by a Valkyrie offering a cup of mead.

in fear. Odin will seek counsel at the Well of Knowledge. The gods, in company with the human heroes gathered over the ages in Valhalla (see pp.132–3), will take up arms and proceed to the battlefield to confront the foe.

In the battle itself, Freyr will be cut down by Surt's flaming sword. Thor will kill Jormungand but will then collapse, poisoned by the serpent's venom. Odin will fall to Fenrir, which will itself be stabbed in the heart by Vidar, the god's son. Tyr will confront Garm, the Hound of Hel, and the two will destroy each other, as will Heimdall and Loki. Then sparks from Surt's brand will set fire to the earth. The sun will be darkened, the firmament will split open, and the stars will fall from the sky. The ocean will break its bounds and the earth will sink into the sea.

Yet life will continue beyond the final cataclysm. A fresh earth will emerge to replace the lost one, and a new and brighter sun will rise in the sky. Two of Odin's sons will survive, as will two of Thor's; and they will be joined by Hod and Baldur, released from Hel at last. In Midgard too a couple will live through the holocaust, hidden in Hodmimir's Wood—from their children the earth will be repeopled. And yet, in the *Völuspá*'s vision, the seeds of evil will be present even in this new age of innocence; the seeress's last words before she falls silent tell of a winged dragon risen from the depths, bearing on its pinions the corpses of dead men.

THE RESTLESS SPIRIT

Even at home, the Norse people were enthusiastic travellers. In summer they moved around on foot or on horseback; in winter they used skates, sledges, and skis. But it was their skill in shipbuilding and sailing that took them to the confines of the known world. The initial push was eastward, across the Baltic and then down the Russian rivers—voyages that were dangerous enough, throwing up hostile terrain and lethal rapids. Yet such inland journeys paled in comparison with the perils of the westward route across the Atlantic, which pitted sailors in open boats equipped with only rudimentary navigational tools against storms, reefs, icebergs, and all the terrors of uncharted seas.

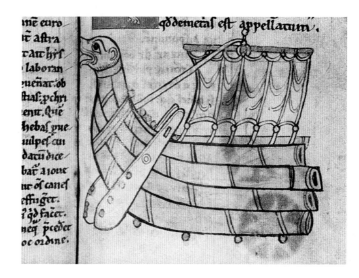

CONQUEST AND PLUNDER

Vikings who set off to seek their fortunes overseas were driven by the same motives that have always inspired adventurers: the desire for land, wealth, and fame. Land hunger was a permanent feature of Scandinavian life—more marked in some areas, such as western Norway, than in others—that continued to drive emigrants abroad up to modern times. Although it seems to have been less extensive in the Viking era than in the earlier Age of Migrations, when whole peoples including Goths, Vandals, Lombards, and Burgundians had headed south, it remained an influential force. The typical Viking raider was a younger son, stout and well-nourished on the high-protein meat-and-dairy diet of the north, eager to find himself an inheritance to match the family estate that would be his elder brother's by birthright.

A detail from the Bayeux Tapestry, woven to commemorate the Norman conquest of England in 1066, shows Duke William's fleet en route across the English Channel. Most of the early Norse raids were small-scale affairs, but large expeditions became more common in later years.

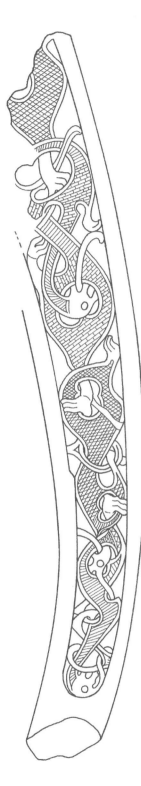

In the course of the Viking Age, the underlying demographic pressures were exacerbated by political developments, and in particular by the rise of national monarchies. For example, in Norway, much of the westward expansion of colonists seeking new lands coincided with King Harald Fairhair's successful campaign around the turn of the ninth and tenth centuries to impose royal control on the independently minded local aristocracy. Many of the original settlers of Iceland and the north Atlantic islands were Norwegians who left their homeland to escape Harald's heavy hand.

By that stage, a century into the Viking Age, the westward routes had already been well charted by earlier generations of pioneers. Yet even the first wave of explorers had been able to draw on a substantial pool of geographical knowledge. Both eastward via the Baltic and westward via the Atlantic, the age of expansion was preceded by a century or more of increasing trade contacts, which had made the Norse peoples more aware than ever before of both the wealth and the accessibility of foreign parts. Even the very first raiders—those who fell upon Holy Island in 793 CE—knew where they were going and what they could expect to find. That information could presumably only have come from traveling merchants, the warriors' non-violent precursors.

Yet if the northern peoples—and particularly young, bold, landless males—had the knowledge and the motive to undertake foreign adventures, they also needed the means to fulfill their ambitions. That was provided by the development of fast, maneuverable ocean-going boats. The longship is rightly regarded as the symbol of the Viking Age; fully developed by the late eighth century, it gave the Norse peoples the tool they needed to take on the world.

This limestone end-slab from an 11th-century tomb was found in St. Paul's churchyard, London, in 1852. Although purely Norse in style, it was probably carved in England to commemorate a follower of King Knut (Canute), the Dane who ruled a North Sea empire from 1016 to 1035.

LONGSHIPS OF VALHALLA

Viking longships are among the loveliest boats ever built, yet their beauty was always strictly utilitarian in the eyes of those who sailed in them. Everything that is pleasing to the eye in their design also contributed to making them the most efficient ocean-going craft the world had yet seen.

Longships, built for war and travel, were far from being the only boats of the Viking Age. As important were the *knarrs*—cargo ships that were broader in the beam, with a length-to-breadth ratio averaging 4:1 in contrast to the longship's 7:1; the extra width amidships provided room for a central, sunken cargo hold. Unlike the longships, *knarrs* were essentially sailing boats with fixed masts; although there were a few oar-ports on the short stretches of decking at either end of the hold, these would only have been used when the ship was becalmed or maneuvering close to shore.

In contrast, the longships had masts that could easily be lowered, whether to reduce wind resistance and improve stability when the craft was being rowed or else to present a low profile for surprise attacks. Sail was the normal method of propulsion on the open sea, but on rivers and in inshore waters the boats were powered by oar.

The combination of sail and oar was the secret of the longship's success. It was only in the period immediately preceding Viking times that northern shipbuilders had mastered the art of providing vessels with tall masts and the concomitant strong keels. The keel was very much the backbone of Viking ships of all kinds; hulls were built outward from it, employing planks of green wood cut

A detail from a Gotland picture stone shows warriors setting off on a raid in a square-rigged longship. Shields were often fixed to the sides of vessels for convenient storage at sea, particularly during ocean-going voyages when oars were little used.

radially in thin wedges from the tree trunk. Much care was taken to work with the grain of the wood; the keel itself would be cut from a single straight trunk, while the ribs would be shaped from limbs and branches that naturally approximated the curve required. The goal was lightness and pliability; the strakes were shaved thin with axes for maximum flexibility, for the hulls were expected to ride the waves, not to fight against them. A good-sized warship would have required the timber of about a dozen oaks (although some, especially in the north, were of pine).

The end result was a vessel of extraordinary strength and navigability. Experiments with modern replicas have shown that longships could achieve speeds of over 10 knots (11.5 miles/18.5 km per hour) in good conditions, and over long distances could average 125 miles (200 km) or more in 24 hours. The combination of oar and sail also made them uniquely adaptable, fitting them for raiding far down rivers while also opening horizons on a wider maritime world.

A model of the celebrated Oseberg ship (see p.107) emphasizes the vessel's sleek lines and shallow draft. The ship was discovered in 1904 near the Oslo Fjord just 10 miles (16 km) from Gokstad, where another famous vessel, also used for a royal burial, had been found 24 years previously (see p.84).

SHIPBUILDING

Viking ships were for the most part built to a regular pattern. They were constructed from the keel upward through a succession of overlapping ("clinker-built") strakes. Fore and aft, curved stems continued the line of the keel, rising up to the prow and sternposts, which were sometimes elaborately decorated. The mast slotted into a heavy timber known as the keelson that was horizontally attached along the center of the vessel.

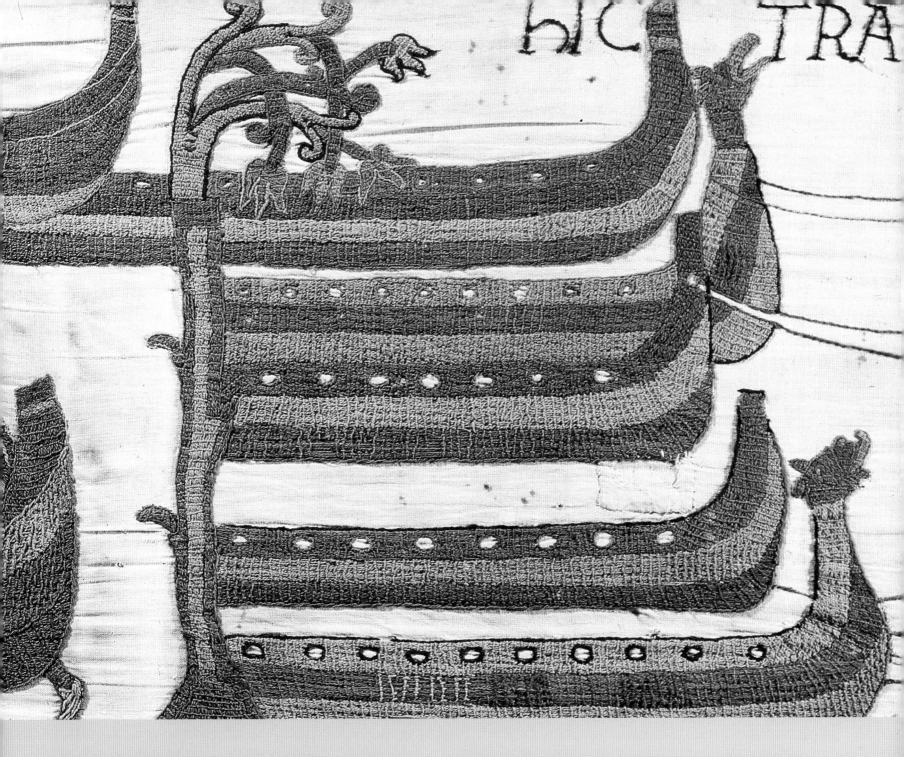

HIC TRA

As shown in the illustration above—a detail from the Bayeux Tapestry depicting the preparation of Duke William of Normandy's invasion fleet—the chief tool employed by shipwrights was the ax, which the men in the foreground are using even for the final trimming of the strakes. Immediately behind them, an overseer assesses the lines of the vessel as a whole. In the background another worker planes the sides of a boat, while his companion uses a T-shaped auger to drill holes for nails in the planking.

DECORATED FOR VALOR

Kings and leading noblemen sought to cut a dash by expensively decorating the
grandest of their longships. Some boats bore bronze weathervanes that were
masterpieces of the metalworker's art, elaborately adorned with writhing
mythological beasts entwined in serpentine patterns. However, the ornamentation
usually took the form of decorated fore- and aft-stems standing proudly at the
boat's prow and stern. "Here there were glittering men of solid gold or silver nearly
comparable to live ones," wrote one observer rhapsodically, describing an eleventh-
century Danish fleet; "there, bulls with necks raised high and legs outstretched,
leaping and roaring just as if they were alive." In Iceland, the martial message of
such bow ornaments was regarded as cause for alarm; one of the nation's earliest
laws prohibited vessels from approaching land "with gaping heads and yawning
jaws, so that the spirits of the land grow frightened at them."

THE WATERY ROAD

A boulder serves to weigh
down a Viking-era anchor.
Both stone and iron
anchors have been found;
usually they were fixed to
boats with ropes rather
than chains. Often they
were not needed;
crews simply drew
their vessels directly
up onto the shore.

In an age when most people never journeyed further than the nearest market town, Viking mariners traversed oceans and crossed continents. Once their shipwrights had mastered the art of building ocean-going vessels, they could regularly cover distances that would have been unthinkable on the muddy, potholed tracks which land travelers had to tackle in their day.

Even so, the vast majority of sea voyages throughout the Viking period were coastal, as they had been in preceding centuries. Such land-hugging trips precluded the need for sophisticated navigation; the helmsman simply followed the shoreline to his destination, keeping a look-out along the way for familiar landmarks that would show how far he had gone. At nightfall he could beach his craft, a relatively easy task thanks to the shallow draft of Viking vessels. There was no need to take bulky supplies aboard, as food and drink would be available at stops along the way.

Even journeys across the sea were not necessarily much more complicated. At its shortest, the crossing from Denmark to northern England took no more than 36 hours, and from there it was possible to travel on to the furthest parts of Ireland without ever losing sight of land. As the Viking Age progressed, the Norse peoples established a network of coastal havens along the most traveled routes, where ships could stop to replenish their supplies; the island of Noirmoutier off France's Atlantic coast was an early example, as were the various Norwegian settlements down the Irish littoral.

However, journeys into the Atlantic to Iceland and Greenland presented challenges of an altogether different order, involving the prospect of several days and nights at sea. By day there was little for most of the crew to do except bale out the

water that seeped through the caulking of moss or tarred animal hair filling the joins in the boat's planking. For food there would be dried fish or meat and unleavened bread; for drink, water from skin bags, or else sour milk or beer. At night, voyagers snatched what sleep they could stretched out between the thwarts under animal-hide blankets, or perhaps huddled for warmth into two-man sleeping bags.

On these open-sea voyages, navigation was a serious challenge for those setting the vessels' course. In place of rudders, the boats had oars attached to the right-hand side near the stern; the English word "starboard" derives from the Old Norse *styra*, meaning "to steer." Although various ingenious theories have been put forward to explain how Viking pilots could have found their way, there is in fact little hard archaeological evidence to suggest that they used any special instruments; their usual methods were dead reckoning and careful observation of natural phenomena, primarily the position of the sun and the Pole Star. One possible exception is a semi-circular piece of wood marked with a regular pattern of notches around its

The placid waters of Iceland's Lake Myvatn belie the violent geothermal activity of the surrounding region. So much of the island consisted of volcanic mountains, lava beds, glaciers, and stony moraines that less than 20 percent of the total land area was available for settlement.

rim; found in Greenland in 1948, it might conceivably have formed part of a solar compass, used to judge direction from a reading taken on the sun's position at noon.

Mostly, though, navigators relied on land- and seamarks to tell them where they were. A medieval description of the journey from Norway to Greenland suggests the kind of thing they were looking out for. "From Hernar you should sail due west to reach Hvarf in Greenland. The route takes you north of Shetland, which can only be seen if the visibility is very good. You will pass south of the Faroes, where the sea appears halfway up the mountain slopes, and so far south of Iceland that you will only know of its presence from the birds and whales off its shores." Other clues for the experienced sailor included iceblink—the reflected glare of a distant ice field in the sky—and the changing wave formations as the seabed shelved up and land drew near.

Life on long sea journeys was always challenging and sometimes a test of endurance. Many a Viking sailor must have shared the sentiments expressed in the roughly contemporaneous Anglo-Saxon poem *The Seafarer*:

> *Endlessly careworn I have coursed my keel / Over furled foam, I forward in the prow /*
> *Numb with cold in the long night watches / Carefully kenning the cliffs we coasted. /*
> *Chill nailed down my feet, frost / Tightened its clamps. Sorrows sighed about my heart /*
> *And hunger made me sick of the sea.*

Yet there were also many consolations for the bold and venturesome. For all its perils, the sea was the path to riches, offering possibilities of adventure that stay-at-homes would never know in a lifetime of drudgery on the soil. It opened the gateway to far horizons, and as such it haunted the Norse imagination, constantly tempting the young and restless with prospects of a better life beyond the waves.

ABOVE A sizeable fleet of late-Viking longships lines up in array in this impromptu wood carving dating from the 12th or 13th century. Some of the vessels have dragon heads on their prows, indicating that they were probably warships; others bear weathervanes.

LORDS OF THE VOLGA

A 12th-century silver pendant, found in a hoard unearthed in Kiev in 1906, suggests the wealth of the Rus state set up by Norse settlers in conjunction with local Slav peoples in the 9th century. The pendant would have been worn suspended from a headdress or crown.

The Vikings who steered east across the Baltic required rather different boats from those who sailed the North Sea. In the East the main trade routes were river-borne, and for this inland traffic lighter vessels were needed that could, when necessary, be portaged overland between headwaters or around rapids.

The lure that drew the merchants into Russia was Arab silver. Of the two main routes, the one down the Volga led first to the trading emporium of Bulgar, then on through the empire of the Khazars, a Turkic people who controlled much of the southern steppes, to the Caspian Sea and the heartland of the Abbasid caliphs beyond. From the Caspian's southern shores, Baghdad itself was a 400-mile (650-km) caravan journey away. This was the capital of the mighty Harun al-Rashid, an *Arabian Nights*-like realm of fabulous wealth, much of it drawn from the silver mines of Transoxiana and Afghanistan.

Norse merchants traded furs, weapons, and slaves for fine Arabian silver coins, which had the double advantage of being precious and easily portable, both essential requirements for traders who traveled light. Back home, the silver transformed the economy; much was melted down to make jewelry, yet even so more than 85,000 surviving coins have been found in hoards, 95 percent of them in Sweden.

Merchants who chose the Dnieper route faced a 1,400-mile (2,250-km) journey to the Black Sea, whose western shores they could then follow to Constantinople, capital of the Byzantine empire. The hazards awaiting them were memorably described by the emperor Constantine Porphyrogenitus. He reported that traders would

Learning about Viking ships through hands-on experience, a group of Danish youths steer a miniature replica of a dragon ship across a river. Viking shipbuilders made smaller versions of the ocean-going vessels for inland travel, though a punt-like flat-bottomed ferry has also been found.

gather in Kiev each June, when the winter meltwaters had subsided; they would travel in large groups, seeking safety in numbers. The passage to the Black Sea took at least six weeks, and crossed seven rapids known by evocative names, including Gulper, Yeller, Seether, Courser, and Ever-Noisy. Some of these could only be traversed by carrying the boats overland, at the risk of attack from hostile local peoples. One, though, could be negotiated with difficulty on foot: Constantine reported that some of the boat's company would be left on shore while the rest stripped naked and reentered the water, "testing the bottom with their feet so as not to stumble over stones." Using poles to steer the vessels they would edge through the rapids, keeping close to the bank, before picking up the rest of the crew and continuing.

It took courage and endurance to make money on the Russian route, and not all who set out returned. A monument to one who did not still stands on the Baltic island of Gotland. Raised by four brothers in memory of a fifth, it states simply, "They went far into Ever-Noisy"—and there, in one of the most fearsome of the Dnieper cataracts, the young man presumably died, many miles from home.

THE NORSEMEN AND THE CITY
To Norse travelers it was Mikligardr, the Great City. With its half-a-million polyglot inhabitants, Constantinople—whose ancient walls are shown here—had no parallel in western Europe at the time.

Although it lay many months' traveling away, the Byzantine capital acted as a magnet for ambitious Norse merchants, who could exchange their wares there for silks, spices, jewelry, and all the luxuries of the Levantine world. Inevitably, such wealth also attracted

Vikings seeking to get rich by less peaceful means. On two occasions, in 860 and 907, raiders sought to breach the city's mighty defenses. Both assaults were eventually driven back, but the defenders were so impressed by the courage and ferocity of their assailants that, once peace had been restored, Norse mercenaries won an honored place in the Byzantine army. Before long they even provided the crack troops that formed the emperor's own bodyguard, known from the Old Norse word for "pledge" as the Varangian Guard.

A SEAMLESS FLOW

I f the taste for plunder first drew Vikings across the North Sea, they soon also showed a desire for land on which they could settle down. On the Scottish islands as well as on the Isle of Man and in the Faroes, they found surroundings that recalled those they had left behind at home. Where the land was vacant and fit for agriculture, they set up farmsteads; where it was occupied, they sometimes took possession by force.

From 795 on, raiders regularly sailed round the northern tip of Scotland to attack targets on the Scottish west coast and in Ireland. They must quickly have grown familiar with the Orkney and Shetland islands, which lie en route just 24 hours' sailing from the Norwegian coast. A hoard of Pictish silver, buried for safe-keeping in the Shetlands about the year 800 and excavated in 1958, provides eloquent evidence of the fear the early visitors must have inspired in the local people. Then, at some unspecified moment possibly as late as the tenth century, raiding turned into occupation, and in time the Orkneys were to become the seat of a powerful dynasty of Viking earls.

Placenames in the Orkneys and Shetlands are now almost entirely Norse in derivation, suggesting that the original Pictish population was totally subjugated. However, down the west coast of Scotland, Norse and Gaelic names both occur, indicating greater mixing of the peoples. Further south, the Isle of Man became the headquarters of an important Viking kingdom that came to include Kintyre and most of Scotland's western islands. Today the Manx people retain many memories of their Viking heritage, including a degree of autonomy and their own parliament, the Tynwald, whose name is an exact linguistic equivalent of the Icelandic *thingvellir*.

The sculpted lines of the Gokstad ship combine beauty and utility in equal measure. The boat's excavation from a Norwegian burial mound in 1880 began the great age of Viking archaeology.

Norse colonists left an even more enduring mark on the Faroe Islands, midway between the Shetlands and Iceland, which remain a dependency of Denmark to this day. The Faroes were unoccupied before the first Norwegian settlers arrived, though not entirely uninhabited; from the early eighth century on they had served as a summertime refuge for Irish monks, who quickly took flight when the first Vikings arrived to disturb their solitude. From the monks or other early travelers, the newcomers inherited flocks of wild sheep; the name Faroes means "Island of Sheep." Along with rich fishing-grounds, good pasturage was in fact the islands' main attraction for the immigrants, some of whom may have found their way there by way of Gaelic-speaking areas; the sagas identify the first arrival as one Grim Kamban, a name that combines Norse and Celtic elements.

The occupation of the Faroes established a Norse presence far out in the North Atlantic, more than 400 miles (650 km) from the Norwegian coast. In time, though, the islands would prove to be stepping stones, like the Orkneys and Shetlands before them, attracting intrepid adventurers to try their luck on even more distant shores.

Waves break against the Old Man of Hoy off the Orkneys, a group of over 70 islands (only about 20 inhabited) off the north of Scotland. Seized by Vikings in the 9th or 10th century, they remained Norse dependencies for more than 600 years until 1472, when they were pawned to the Scottish crown, and have not been redeemed since.

THE ISLAND OF FIRE

Steam rises from fumaroles in Iceland, the world's most geothermally active country. Some early settlers channeled natural hot springs to fill circular open-air baths.

Proof if such were needed that Viking navigation was an approximate art comes from the first voyages to Iceland. The island was actually discovered twice, each time by sailors blown off course while heading for other destinations. A Norwegian Viking named Naddod found his way there around the year 860 when trying to reach the Faroes; having climbed a snow-covered mountain and seen no sign of life, he sailed away again. At roughly the same time, a Swede called Gardar Svavarsson was blown north while en route for the Hebrides. He was sufficiently impressed by what he found to spend a whole year circumnavigating Iceland's heavily

indented, 35,000-mile (60,000-km) coastline, overwintering at Husavik on the north coast. Then he returned to inhabited parts to report on what he had found.

In a world where land was in short supply, there was an eager audience for news of virgin territory, however forbidding the surroundings might seem to be. Word of the new land's active volcanoes and fields of lava failed to deter would-be settlers, even though much misinformation subsequently spread about them; one later writer claimed that "the ice on account of its age is so black and dry in appearance that it burns when fire is set to it." Iceland was named by one of its first inhabitants, a Norwegian called Floki Vilgerdarson who, according to the sagas, found his way there by using caged birds as navigation aids. The first he released flew back to the Faroes from where he had set out, while the second merely circled and then landed back on the boat; but the third led him westward to his destination. From this Noah-like stratagem the pioneer won the nickname of Raven Floki. However, Floki's stay was not a happy one; he left before a year was out, having lost all his livestock as a result of failing to put hay aside for winter fodder. The unappealing name he chose for the new land no doubt reflected his own bitter experiences there.

However, others succeeded where Floki had failed. Some sailed from the Western Isles of Scotland, bringing Celts with them as slaves; but most came from Norway, many seeking a place where they could be their own masters, free of the threat of royal interference. They traveled in *knarrs*, the workhorses of the westward expansion, whose capacious central holds provided room to store livestock and provisions. Some traveled the 650 miles (1,050 km) from the Norwegian coast directly, setting their course due west; in ideal sailing conditions, the journey could take as little as four days. Others took a more southerly route, making landfalls on the Shetlands and Faroes, which lay about 48 hours' sailing across open ocean from

Carved from a walrus tusk, this sculpture is the work of craftsmen of the Dorset culture, predecessors of the Inuit peoples who already inhabited northwest Greenland at the time when the Norse settlers arrived in the south. Relations between the two communities were very limited until the 14th century, when climate change forced the northern people southward.

The ruins of a medieval church mark the site of Brattahlid, where Eirik the Red settled in 983 when he established the first Norse colony in Greenland. From Brattahlid his son Leif Eiriksson set out 18 years later to make the earliest known European landfall in North America.

Iceland's south-eastern point. Either way the colonists faced a risky crossing, exposed to the unpredictable perils of Atlantic storms. Those who survived the journey settled on fertile grazing land, building turf-walled farmhouses such as the one reconstructed at Stöng to the south-east of Thingvellir (see pp.108–9).

By about the year 930, all the available farming land in Iceland had been claimed, and pioneers seeking fresh horizons had to start looking further afield. One man who had strong personal reasons for doing so was a certain Eirik the Red. Forced to flee Norway for Iceland after the killing of two adversaries in a family feud, Eirik also got into trouble in his new home, where there were fresh disputes

with neighbors and more killings. Eventually Eirik was sentenced to three years' banishment by order of the Althing. Rather than heading for the Faroes or Ireland as most people in his position would have done, he set his mind to investigating a story that had been circulating in Iceland for a half century or more. This told how one Gunnbjorn Ulf-Krakason had been blown off course while sailing from Norway to Iceland. Before turning east to regain his destination, he had sighted a huge, rocky landmass in uncharted seas far to the west.

Eirik set out with a boatload of companions in the year 982 to find this land, and after traveling across some 450 miles (750 km) of open ocean they duly did so. At first sight the discovery looked unpromising; the coastline that met their eyes offered only sheer cliffs dropping from a gigantic icecap. But the travelers turned south, rounding the tip of the landmass, and on the western coast they found sheltered fjords flanked by rich pasture. There they made their home.

When Eirik's banishment was up, he and his companions returned to Iceland with dazzling stories of the lushness of the new land. With an eye to attracting colonists, Eirik called his discovery Greenland, reckoning shrewdly that "people would be drawn to go there if it had an attractive name." A year later he set out again, this time not as an exile but as a founding father at the head of a fleet of 25 ships, 14 of which survived the Atlantic storms to reach their destination. The 400 men and women aboard formed the foundation of a Viking colony that was to survive not just through the Viking Age but also for most of the Middle Ages as well, finally dying out sometime in the fifteenth century after a continuous history of almost 500 years.

Worsening relations with Greenland's Inuit population helped bring about the final demise of the Greenland settlement in the 15th century. Here a 19th-century Inuit artist has portrayed one incident in the spiraling conflict between the peoples.

ON VINLAND'S SHORES

The final stepping stone in the Vikings' expansion across the Atlantic was North America itself. The first sighting of the North American coast came around the year 986 from a mariner named Bjarni

Herjofsson who had missed the way to Greenland. Another 15 years passed before the first landfall was made by Eirik the Red's son Leif Eiriksson, who had bought Bjarni's boat and retraced his route. The region where Leif and his companions overwintered was Vinland,

whose name probably derives from the Old Norse "vin," meaning field or meadow. Leif's glowing account on his return to Greenland inspired Thorfinn Karlsefni to launch a full-scale attempt at colonization a few years later, but the hostility of the native peoples—possibly Inuit, but more likely Algonquins—drove the 250 settlers back to Greenland after less than three years. Thereafter Greenlanders continued to make occasional visits in search of timber, which their own land lacked; the last recorded trip was in 1347.

BELIEF AND RITUAL

LEFT A dragon ship goes up in flames at the annual Up-Helly-Aa festival in the Shetland Isles north of mainland Scotland. Although Up-Helly-Aa itself dates back only to the 1870s, there is evidence that a midwinter ceremony was held in the Norse lands in Viking times to ensure the success of the following year's crops.

The Viking world did not separate the religious from the secular. The old Norse gods had no priests, and there is little evidence for the existence of purpose-built places of worship. Instead, religious observances suffused the fabric of everyday life and rituals were often performed in the open air. Kings, earls, and other prominent men presided over the seasonal ceremonies at which entire communities offered support to the gods; but much impromptu worship also took place informally in the humbler confines of the home or farmstead. There were also other, darker traditions of divination (*seid*)—of wise men and women with prophetic powers—that were largely, although not entirely, swept away with the coming of Christianity as the Viking Age drew to a close.

BELOW A scene scratched on stone shows a Christian missionary welcoming a convert to the new faith. The gradual adoption of Christianity in the Norse lands in the course of the 10th and 11th centuries destroyed the worship of the old gods and effectively marked the end of the Viking Age.

GIFTS FOR THE GODS

Sacrifice was central to Norse religion, and it took many forms. The most structured rituals took place at seasonal turning-points and involved entire communities. The usual venue was the great hall of the local lord or ruler, around which the blood of a slaughtered animal would be strewn by way of consecration; the sacrifice was the prologue to a feast (see pp.96–7) at which the carcass would be eaten.

The greatest of all such gatherings probably took place at Uppsala in Sweden and at Lejre in Denmark. Both ceremonies are known only from Christian writers who may have distorted the proceedings, yet there are remarkable similarities between the two accounts. Each festival was held every nine years, and both human and animal sacrifices were offered up. The number nine had obvious cultic significance, for at Lejre there were said to be 99 human victims, along with similar numbers of horses, dogs, and cocks, while at Uppsala nine males of every available species including humans, to a total of 72, were killed—the corpses hung in a sacred grove. All of Sweden's provinces were represented, with individuals of note either attending in person or else sending gifts, although Christians, who abhorred the proceedings, were allowed to buy exemptions.

The events at Uppsala and Lejre appear to have been in every way exceptional; most sacrificial rites were on a much smaller scale and were more personal in their goals. So Rus traders traveling down the Volga would set up wooden statues of the gods and sacrifice sheep and cattle to them to solicit good trading. In Scandinavia itself, offerings were made not just to the major deities but also to the spirits thought to inhabit

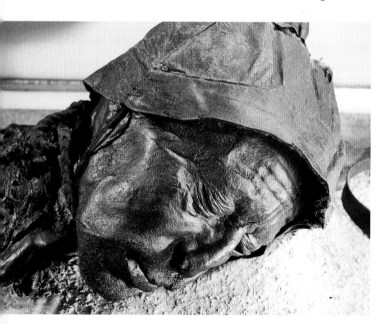

Long before Viking times, people were apparently offered up for sacrifice in the Norse lands. Discovered in a peat bog near Tollund, Denmark, in 1950, this man was naked but for a belt and cap, with the leather rope used to hang or strangle him still in place around his neck. He was sacrificed in about 200 BCE.

These trees at Old Uppsala in Sweden may stand on the site of the sacred grove featured in the most celebrated of all the Norse peoples' sacrificial ceremonies. In its course, according to the chronicler Adam of Bremen, the bodies of as many as 72 human and animal victims were strung up, and "each and every tree is considered divine because of the victims' death and putrefaction."

groves, rocks, and waterfalls. One eleventh-century Christian poet described being turned away from a farmstead where he had sought shelter for the night because the farmer's wife was sacrificing to the local elves.

Individual deities favored certain types of offering. Odin's victims were usually hanged—he was Lord of the Gallows—or killed with a spear, his sacred weapon; stallions and boars were offered up to the fertility god Freyr. Artifacts as well as living beings were acceptable—large caches of ritually damaged weapons have been recovered from lakes, bogs, and other sites. Whatever the offering, the purpose seems to have been the same: to win divine favor in return for something of value.

THE CEREMONIAL FEAST

Feasting was closely related to sacrifice in the Viking world; in all the major seasonal ceremonies, both played a part. When circumstances demanded, any location could be chosen. Such was the case of the Danish warriors discovered by Irish monks celebrating their triumph against Norwegian Vikings outside Dublin in 852 CE; to the visitors' horror, they had set their cauldrons upon the piled bodies of the Norwegian dead.

More typical practice was to celebrate feasts in halls that had been swept clean and decorated festively for the occasion, perhaps with wall hangings. Large amounts

Kings and warriors would have drunk toasts from vessels like this beautiful silver cup, found on the Danish island of Fejø and dated to about the year 800. Feasting played a central part in the old Norse religion, accompanying sacrifices and reaffirming ties of loyalty and shared culture.

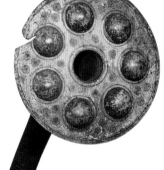

of ale or mead, the principal drinks, would have been prepared in advance and ritually hallowed to the gods. The flesh of the sacrificial animal might be roasted over a spit or stewed, and to accompany it there would be fish, gruel, bread, and vegetables, along with fruit, berries, and nuts. The diners would sit on benches at long tables, carousing by the light of oil lamps, flaming torches, and a fire blazing in a central hearth.

An important part of the proceedings was the drinking of toasts to dead ancestors and to the gods—these would be proposed by the leading figure present. The ale would circulate in great metal-rimmed drinking horns passed from hand to hand among the guests; two such, taken from aurochs, were found in the Sutton Hoo burial site in East Anglia, England. Besides eating and drinking, there would be other entertainments: musicians would play on lyres and flutes; poets would recite verses about the myths; and storytellers would recount the epic deeds of heroes and gods.

Such feasts had a significance that went far beyond mere conviviality. They were an opportunity for host and guests to reaffirm the ties that bound them together. They gave chiefs a chance to reward their retainers not just with their hospitality but also with more tangible gifts, particularly rings and other valuables. Above all they served to celebrate a common culture, as illustrated by a cautionary tale of King Hakon, who sought to bring Christianity to Norway in the tenth century. According to the Icelandic poet and chronicler Snorri Sturluson, writing two centuries later, the ruler deeply offended his pagan subjects by participating only half-heartedly in the important annual Winter Nights festival. To stave off open revolt he eventually had to compromise his Christian principles to the extent of eating a little of the meat of the stallion sacrificed there in honor of the old gods.

Dating from the Bronze Age, lurs were ceremonial horns, typically about 4 ft (1.2 m) long, that produced mournful, trombone-like sounds. Rock carvings indicate that they were used in religious rites, but what form these rituals might have taken is not known.

MAGIC AND TRANSFORMATION

Magic and transformation both featured strongly in the Norse myths. As in Celtic lore, certain of the gods regularly changed both shape and species in order to conceal their real identity and achieve their goals. In pursuit of the Mead of Inspiration, Odin took on the form of a serpent to worm his way into the cellar where the divine draft was kept. Loki adopted the guise of a falcon to regain the Apples of Youth from the giant who had stolen them, and changed himself into a seal to escape Odin's wrath after stealing the priceless Brisingamen necklace from Freyja. Freyja also was said to have the power to change into a falcon.

The gods not only had the power to alter their own shapes, but those of others too. On one of their occasional forays into Midgard, Odin, Loki, and Honir tested their magical powers against those of the giant Skrymsli when he came, in ogre fashion, to take and eat the son of their human hosts. First Odin shrank the boy so that he was small enough to hide in an ear of corn, and then Honir transformed him into a feather on a swan's neck, but each time Skrymsli tracked him down. Loki finally saved the boy, first by turning him into a single egg in a fish's roe, and then, when even that failed, by trapping Skrymsli in quicksand in which he duly drowned.

Other powers exercised by the gods included that of bringing the dead back to life. Thor had the ability to restore his two goats, Tooth-gnasher and Tooth-gritter, after killing and eating them; the twist in the tale was that the bones had to be intact for the magic to work. According to the story, some marrow had been extracted from one of them, causing that particular goat to limp when revived.

Other beings besides gods also had magical powers. Giants could take on

LEFT **This golden trefoil brooch from 9th-century Norway would have served to fasten a rich person's cloak or shawl. In pursuit of wealth, love, or vengeance, individuals in Viking times sometimes had recourse to the potent form of magic known as** *seid.*

RIGHT **In the misty distance mountains glimmer on the Lofoten Islands, north of the Norwegian mainland. Viking Age inhabitants of more southerly parts of Scandinavia tended to associate the far north with magic, a belief that may have had its origins in the shamanistic practices of the region's Saami inhabitants.**

e Metamorphofi hominum in Lupo

Belief in the power of magic lingered on after the end of the Viking Age. In his 16th-century work on Scandinavia, the geographer Olaus Magnus chose to portray the region as the haunt of demons and witches, describing various occult practices including the transformation of humans into wolves.

animal form just as the deities could—the storm giant Thiassi turned himself into an eagle to pursue Loki in falcon shape as he brought Iduna and the golden apples back to Asgard. So too could certain humans, to judge from the start of the *Volsung* saga; the entire tragedy of the Sigurd legend was set in motion when Loki killed an otter that turned out to be the son of a powerful magician; the youth had chosen to assume that shape to hunt fish.

The shape-shifting in Norse myth inevitably brings to mind the world of the shamans—individuals credited in many cultures with powers that included the ability to transform themselves into animals. Shamanism was common to most of the peoples of northern Eurasia. The most likely channel into the Norse world was through the Saami or Lapps, Arctic neighbors of the Norwegians and Swedes. There are in fact hints in the histories that the remote regions where the Saami lived were regarded with a superstitious awe; the chronicler Snorri Sturluson reported that the beautiful wife of Norway's tenth-century king Eirik Bloodax, who came from the far north, was deeply versed in magic.

Yet the most feared form of magic in the Norse world may well have had other roots. Called *seid*, it was generally malicious in intent, and it was connected in the popular imagination with the Vanir. Its actual origins may be hinted at in one of the most enigmatic of the myths—that concerning the cause of the conflict between the Aesir and the Vanir (see pp.40–41). According to the *Völuspá*, the dispute began when the Aesir tortured a certain Gullveig, piercing her with spears and then burning her without being able to kill her. The Vanir then took up arms in her defense, and the world's first war began.

Gullveig is mentioned nowhere else in the myths and her identity is uncertain. However, the name means "love of gold," an attribute she shared with the principal Vanir goddess Freyja, who was famously fond of golden jewelry and who was said to weep tears of gold. If Freyja and Gullveig were indeed one and the same person, it may be that *seid* was associated from the beginning with her cult and represented a major cause of conflict between the worshipers of the two different sets of deities when their respective cults first came into contact.

Whatever its origins, *seid* continued to be respected and feared in equal measure throughout the Viking Age. While female seers could make legitimate use of it to obtain powers of prophecy (see pp.104–5), male practitioners were bitterly condemned; one chronicle reports that King Harald Fairhair of Norway, father of Eirik Bloodax, set fire to the home of one of his other sons to punish him for resorting to *seid*; the youth was burned alive together with 80 of his followers.

Like their Celtic contemporaries, the Norse peoples favored a style of art in which identity was fluid: mythical beasts might transmute into foliate patterns, and abstract designs turn out to have animal heads. This detail of a 7th-century shield furnishing from Norway suggests some fantastical bird's beak.

THE MYSTIC SPIRAL

One distinctive feature of Norse design is a circular disc filled either with whirling black and white curves or else with spiral patterns. In either case the impression given is one of movement—that of a turning wheel. The most memorable representations are found on stones from the Swedish island of Gotland, raised from the early centuries of the first millennium CE up until about the year 1000 to commemorate the dead. There have been various attempts to explain the significance of the patterns, which carry a visual impact similar to that of the 1960s op-art paintings they sometimes call to mind. The discs are generally interpreted as surviving symbols of a Bronze Age sun cult whose influence once stretched across much of southern Scandinavia.

OMEN AND PROPHECY

Some practitioners of *seid* had special status in the Norse world. These were the female seers known as *volvas*, who passed from house to house predicting the fortunes of individuals and of entire communities.

The only detailed account of a *volva* at work comes from a late source—the thirteenth-century *Eirik the Red's Saga*—and sets the events in Greenland, though the customs it describes probably reflect earlier Norwegian models. As the saga tells the story, the *volva* journeyed as an honored guest from farmstead to farmstead, offering advice on everything from marriage prospects to the likely outcome of the next harvest. She dressed spectacularly in an outfit fashioned from many different animal skins—reminiscent of the feather cloak that Freyja lent to Loki to give him powers of flight—and carried a brass staff. Sitting on a high seat to deliver her predictions, she started the consultation by consuming a meal made from the hearts of sacrificial animals. Entering a trance while a young girl chanted a spell, she then proceeded to answer questions about the girl's prospects and those of various other interlocutors in her audience. According to the saga, most of her predictions duly came to pass.

Although the sources leave it uncertain how common such figures were in real life, the *volvas* certainly made their mark in literature and myth. The poem called the *Völuspá*, our major source for Norse ideas of the beginning and end of the world, is presented in the form of the visions of just such a seeress, consulted by Odin who paid her with bracelets and necklaces. And when the beautiful god Baldur was troubled by

The *volvas*—itinerant prophetesses of the Norse world—carried staffs as symbols of their authority. This birdlike metal figurine dates back to the late Bronze Age, more than a millennium before the Viking era began, but it too was used to top a staff and may have had some ritual significance.

premonitions of looming disaster, myth recounts that Odin traveled to the gates of Hel itself to consult another prophetess, this one long dead—the god had to use the dark art of necromancy to resuscitate her temporarily.

Not all such prophets were women. There are references in the sagas to male seers foretelling the future at sacrificial feasts. Warrior leaders too were expected to have skill in augury, studying the flight of birds in order to interpret dreams and omens and draw lessons about the likely outcome of their actions. In addition, Viking bands practiced sortilege; according to the ninth-century *Life of Anskar*, one group decided to abandon a planned attack on the trading center of Birka when the lots they drew predicted a negative outcome.

Now purely pastoral, this site on the island of Björkö, 20 miles (32 km) west of present-day Stockholm, was once the seat of Birka, the bustling entrepot of the Vikings' eastern and western trade routes. A 9th-century chronicle tells how the town was saved from attack on one occasion by the drawing of lots.

IN PURSUIT OF FERTILITY

RIGHT Among the grave goods found with the Oseberg ship (opposite) was a wagon whose carved decorations include this enigmatic scene. It shows a woman restraining a knife-wielding man from striking at a rider on horseback.

BELOW With its stick-figure lovers ringed by a circle of ears of corn, this lid of a funerary urn from Bronze Age Denmark obviously links sexual and agricultural fertility—in Viking times both concerns of the Vanir family of gods.

Fertility in the Norse world was associated with the Vanir, the family of gods dominated by Njord and his twin children Freyr and Freyja. There are also references in the literature to an allied cult of the *disir* or goddesses, tutelary spirits of households and of features of the landscape to whom sacrifices were offered at the time of the Winter Nights festival. Freyja is sometimes referred to as Vanadis, *dis* (goddess) of the Vanir, and Freyr similarly received offerings at the Winter Nights, so it is likely that the two forms of worship went hand in hand.

An intriguing glimpse of northern fertility rites in pre-Viking times comes in a famous passage from the Roman historian Tacitus (ca. 56–ca. 120 CE), describing the religious practices of peoples in Denmark and northern Germany in the first century CE. He refers to the cult of a goddess named Nerthus, the linguistic equivalent of the (male) Vanir god Njord. According to

Tacitus, Nerthus's chief shrine was in a sacred grove on an island, probably in the Baltic Sea, where her image was kept under wraps in a wagon. When the presiding priest sensed that the goddess herself was present, the wagon would be hitched to oxen and led out through the surrounding countryside. Warriors would lay down their weapons as she passed, for she was an Earth Mother, a goddess of peace. Yet she also inspired fear, for when the wagon returned to the sacred grove, the slaves who ritually cleansed it were drowned as sacrifices to the goddess in the lake where they carried out the task.

Archaeology has provided corroborative evidence for the cult in the form of two magnificently carved wooden wagons recovered from a Danish peat bog and dated to the period when Tacitus was writing. There are also indications that memories of the cult might have continued into the Viking Age. The great Oseberg ship burial bore the corpses of two women, one aged about 50, the other 30; to judge from the quality of the grave goods buried with them, at least one of the women must have been of the highest rank. Among the finest of the items that accompanied them into the afterlife was a wheeled wagon with a long yoke, suitable for drawing by horses or oxen. Not only was the vehicle of just the type that must have been used to carry the image of Nerthus; its richly carved body was also designed to be lifted off the vehicle's chassis, possibly for transportation by boat but also conceivably for easy immersion and cleansing.

Restored after 1,000 years in the earth, the Oseberg boat now rests in Oslo's Viking Ship Museum. Although it was seaworthy, its low sides and thin keel suggest it was designed for mainly ceremonial use.

THE MEETING PLACE OF THE CHIEFS

The Viking world's best-known secular ceremonial gatherings were the *thing*s, or assemblies of freemen—prototype parliaments that on the Scandinavian mainland came together to elect rulers and settle questions of law. However, the best known today is Iceland's Althing, which met annually from the year 930 on at the spectacular open-air site of Thingvellir (Parliament Plains), before a natural wall of lava in a central region of the country. There representatives of the nation's various districts would gather each midsummer to hear the laws of the land recited and to decide how they should be applied in individual cases. Part supreme court, part legislature, the Althing was a genuinely pioneering institution, Europe's first national, representational parliament.

JEWELRY AND AMULETS

Living in spartan times, the Viking peoples expressed their love of ostentation through jewelry. Men and women alike wore arm- and neckrings as well as shoulder brooches that held their outer garments in place; in addition, women wore necklaces, pendants, and occasionally finger-rings. Plain silver neck- and armrings were made in standard weights so that they could double up as currency; to settle small amounts they were often cut into fragments known as "hack-silver." Most of the metal used was melted down from Middle Eastern coins brought back to Scandinavia by Rus traders.

One Arab observer left an account of these merchant Vikings, whom he encountered on the Volga trade route. "Each of their women," he wrote, "wears on either breast a drum-shaped brooch of iron, silver, copper, or gold whose value indicates how much her husband is worth. The brooches bear rings to which knives can be attached. The women also wear neckrings of gold and silver, but their most prized ornaments are green glass beads that they string together as necklaces."

While most jewelry was worn simply for display, some pieces had a deeper significance. From about 400 to 600 CE, there was a fashion for small pendants made of gold or silver stamped with images often drawn from Norse mythology. These bracteates, as they are now called, were apparently worn for good luck, as were miniature replicas of Thor's Mjollnir (see p.52) some centuries later.

Jewelry also played a part in myth. The Brisingamen necklace caused strife in Asgard, while the cursed golden ring of the dwarf Andvari set in motion the sequence of greed, murder, and revenge that made up the Sigurd legend. In real life, oaths were regularly taken on arm-rings that had been reddened with sacrificial blood; pagan Danes are said to have made peace with England's King Alfred the Great by "swearing oaths to him on the holy ring."

An array of body ornaments indicates the opulence of the Norse metalworkers' craft. The two circular gold brooches, found in Denmark, are dated to about the year 1000. The ring-shaped fastenings are from Sweden, and are now in Stockholm's National Historical Museum.

THE COMING OF CHRISTIANITY

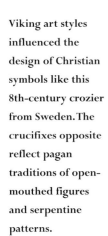

More than any political event, the coming of Christianity marked the end of the Viking Age. Acceptance of the new religion removed the main barrier cutting the Norse countries off from the rest of Europe. By the time the process was complete, at the end of the eleventh century, Scandinavia remained geographically and linguistically distinct, but in other respects was largely integrated into the culture of the continent as a whole.

Christianity's arrival was gradual and piecemeal. As tireless travelers, the Vikings were aware of its presence in other lands long before they accepted it themselves. When it did arrive, its fortunes at first ebbed and flowed with the tide of politics. One Danish king received baptism as early as the year 826, only to be driven into exile the following year. A missionary named Anskar subsequently built churches in leading market towns—at Birka in Sweden as well as Hedeby and Ribe on the Danish mainland. But the conversion of Denmark as a whole had to wait until about the year 965, when King Harald Bluetooth finally adopted the new faith. Reportedly he was won over by a miracle performed by a missionary named Poppo, who donned a red-hot iron glove without burning his hand.

In Norway, conversion came about very much as a matter of *realpolitik*; kings seeking to impose their will on the nation's unruly and independent-minded noblemen saw the Church as a buttress of central authority. The process started when

Viking art styles influenced the design of Christian symbols like this 8th-century crozier from Sweden. The crucifixes opposite reflect pagan traditions of open-mouthed figures and serpentine patterns.

King Harald Fairhair (ca. 880–ca. 930)—the first to unite the nation—sent his son Hakon to England to be fostered by the Christian king Athelstan. Hakon in fact died an apostate, and the new faith was eventually imposed by two Olafs—Olaf Tryggvason, who set out in 995 to convert the country by the sword, and then the ruler remembered as St. Olaf, who completed the work before his death in battle in 1030. One saga recounts that he offered the pagan earls a stark choice: "Be killed, leave the country, or accept baptism."

At approximately the same time, Iceland accepted Christianity under pressure from the Norwegian kings, though there the decision was made democratically by decree of the Althing. The hold-out was Sweden, where the old religion was unusually slow to die. Although the nation's rulers were Christian from the early eleventh century on, the two faiths co-existed for almost a century before the Church finally gained the ascendant.

The wooden stave churches of Norway, built from the 11th century on, include some architectural masterpieces, none finer than this one at Borgund, north of Bergen on the Sognefjord. Some details of its construction may echo features of buildings used for religious purposes in pagan times.

The effects of the switch were gradual but profound, affecting all aspects of Norse culture. Conversion was accompanied by a shift from local hegemony to centralized authority; from an oral culture to one based on writing, above all Holy Scripture; and from a morality of honor and retaliation to one of submission and forgiveness. The new faith was unarguably a civilizing force, yet with its coming something of the heroic individualism of the Viking period died. A new age had been born, and the northern world was never to be quite the same again.

THE SWORD AND THE HELM

One point that all contemporaries of the Vikings agreed upon was that they were fearsome fighters. Foreign chroniclers compared them to wild beasts, stinging hornets, and ravening wolves. Even the nicknames that individual warriors won could be alarming: Eirik Bloodax, Harald Wartooth, Ivar thc Boneless, Thorolf Lousebeard. A stanza by the Icelandic poet and warrior Egil Skalla-Grimsson captured the bloodthirsty tone: *I've been with sword and spear / Slippery with bright blood / Where kites wheeled. And how well / We fierce Vikings clashed! / Red flames ate up men's roofs, / Raging we killed and killed; / And skewered bodies sprawled / Sleepy in town gateways.*

A PEOPLE AT WAR

Warfare in Viking times was still very much a personal affair. As in Homer's day, warriors rallied to the banner of individuals who had won reputations as military leaders. Success bred success—a commander with victories to his name would attract fresh followers, allowing him in turn to acquire yet more booty and fame.

When they first descended on an unwary and unprepared Europe, Norse warbands won a reputation as hit-and-run raiders, and throughout the Viking Age mobility was a key to their success. Command of the sea lanes gave them the inestimable advantage of surprise; they could fall seemingly out of the blue on coastal targets, while the shallow draft of their longships also enabled them to attack up rivers inland. When forced to strike far from their boats, they would commandeer horses to reach their objective fast.

Yet for all the emphasis on speed, the Scandinavians were also familiar with more static forms of warfare. The Danes in particular fought lengthy campaigns in England and in the Frankish lands in which discipline and endurance were more important than rapid-strike tactics. And although the Vikings generally avoided siege warfare, they showed that they knew how to raise ramparts and build siege engines when they did undertake it, as at Paris in 885.

Above all, though, Viking armies excelled in hand-to-hand fighting. A typical encounter would begin with the two forces lined up often only a few hundred yards apart. The warband leader might take the time to address a few words of encouragement to his men, who would respond by hurling insults at the enemy ranks. To start hostilities, the commander sometimes cast a spear—Odin's weapon—over the heads of the opposing army, shouting "Odin take them all!"; the idea was to offer the foe en masse as a sacrifice to the Norse war god. Then a hail

Used both for thrusting and for throwing, the spear was a vital weapon in the Viking armory. Attached to a lengthy shaft, it maximized the advantage of long reach enjoyed by the large Norse warriors, of whom one Arab observer wrote: "I have never known a people so tall; they are as big as palm trees."

of arrows, stones, and javelins would descend on the enemy's heads as the two sides closed on one another.

In close-contact fighting, the Viking soldiers had a crucial advantage: physical size. Brought up on a high-protein diet of meat and dairy foods, they tended to be bigger than their opponents. Measurement of the skeletons in Viking graves suggests that men of fighting age averaged about 5 ft 8 in (1.72 m) in height at a time when the European mean was closer to 5 ft 5 in (1.65 m). In the cut-and-thrust of battle with sword and spear, the Norsemen could count on all the benefits of longer reach that boxers cherish in the ring to this day.

In its day, the fortress of Fyrkat in Jutland was a bustling encampment housing craftsmen as well as soldiers. The fort was one of five, all built in the 980s to an identical plan. Probably commissioned by Denmark's King Harald Bluetooth, it went out of service soon after the end of his reign.

The Vikings were also very conscious of the psychological aspect of battle, doing everything they could to seem formidable in the sight of those they confronted. One tactic was to make a fearsome noise; by rattling arrow-quivers and emitting blood-curdling battle-howls they sought to cow the foe into submission. Some individuals also boosted their confidence by resorting to magic: the Eddic poem the *Hávamál* lists various battle spells used to achieve such ends as blunting an enemy's weapons, making comrades impervious to wounds and stopping arrows in mid-air.

One group of warriors carried such stratagems to extremes, working themselves up into a frenzy that apparently made them immune from pain. These were the berserkers, a lifelong fellowship of fighters who took their name from the bearskin outfits that they sometimes wore. To their adversaries, they must have looked quite horrifying: they rolled their eyes, foamed at the mouth, bit their own shields, and sometimes even fought stark naked, relying on sheer fury and their fighting prowess to prevail. Some probably fought drunk, but others relied merely on the adrenaline rush of combat and maybe also on breathing techniques to reach the necessary state of fearless distraction.

At the heart of any action would be the warband's leader surrounded by his bodyguard, warriors hand-picked for their fighting skills. One would carry the

Silver coins and armrings make up most of a magnificent treasure hoard found on the site of the Viking trading base of Birka in 1872. All but one of the coins originated in the Arab world, underlining Birka's position as the terminus of the eastern trade routes across the Baltic.

standard that marked the chief's position, a favorite target for enemy attack. If the leader decided for any reason to call off the fighting, he would do so by raising his shield. More often, though, the battle would continue until the enemy line broke and the remaining soldiers fled.

Seasoned campaigners grew used to these moments of triumph, and to the harvesting of the spoils of war that usually followed. The sheer volume of loot that the Norsemen acquired in the course of their campaigns is well illustrated by the example of Ireland: in modern times almost as many treasures of eighth-century Irish art have been found in Norway, where the Viking raiders took them, as in Ireland itself where they were created.

Viking forces were not invincible, but defeats were extremely rare occurrences. The only people who were able to tame them were women. For Norse fighting men—unlike the colonists who went to the Faroes and Iceland—generally traveled without their womenfolk, with the result that when they did settle down, as in the English Danelaw in the ninth century, they often ended up marrying into the local population.

The results could be dramatic. When Normandy was settled by Duke Rollo and his followers from the year 910 on, acculturation was so rapid that the children of even the first generation of incomers were almost all brought up speaking French. So marked was the culture shift that, one generation on, Rollo's son William Longsword could find no one in his capital of Rouen to teach his own child the Viking language of Old Norse; he had to send to Bayeux 90 miles (150 km) away to hire a tutor.

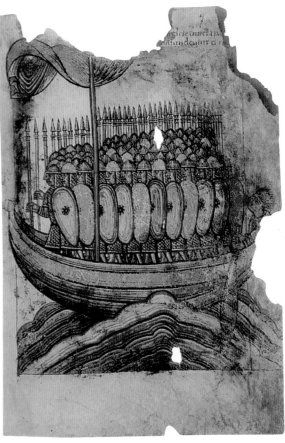

An illustration from a life of St. Aubin shows Vikings preparing to attack the city of Angers, of which he was bishop. The raid took place in the 9th century, but the artist, working 200 or more years later, has anachronistically portrayed the warriors with kite-shaped shields (see p.127).

COMMANDERS OF THE BRAVE

Carved of walrus ivory in the 12th century, these chessmen—a king and two knights—suggest the link between a ruler and his personal guard that lay at the heart of the Viking power structure. The figures form part of a hoard of 93 pieces discovered on the Isle of Lewis in the Outer Hebrides in 1851.

The concept of kingship blossomed in Scandinavia in the course of the Viking Age; the new wealth and complexity of the times fostered the growth of national monarchies, first in Denmark and then in Norway, with Sweden lagging behind. Yet throughout its course royal power remained personal and insecure in all three countries, resting heavily on the charisma and military success of the individual who held the throne.

Norse kings had to be of royal birth, though strict rules of heredity did not necessarily apply; other candidates beside the ruler's eldest son might contend for the throne, increasing the risk of dynastic strife.

Once a king had established his authority, he could only maintain it by *force majeure*, keeping a wary eye on the ambitions of potential rivals. His chief support came from a committed band of armed retainers, who would serve both as his personal bodyguard and as the core of his army in case of war; the individuals who composed it pledged their loyalty by kneeling before him and laying their hands on his sword hilt. In return for their continued allegiance, the ruler would reward them with feasts, lodging, and generous gifts. A poet summed up the relationship succinctly:

> They are favored with wealth and finest swordblades, / With metal from
> Hunland and maids from the East. / Glad are they when they guess battle's
> near, / Swift to leap up and lay hands to their oars.

To ensure the continued support of his warriors, the king needed a regular revenue stream, much of which would come from his own estates; other major sources of income included duties levied on trade and fines paid by criminals, along with the spoils of war. Rather than keeping to one residence, rulers were peripatetic, moving constantly

Warriors line up in file on this 7th-century bronze matrix, thought to have been used to cast metal plaques to decorate helmets. The fighters' own headgear is adorned with stylized boars—animals sacred to Freyr, who was a patron of fighting men as well as a god of fertility.

around their estates and those of leading nobles. Given the violent ends to many reigns, the mood on the royal progresses must often have been wary and mistrustful—this was a world not very far from that of Shakespeare's *Macbeth*.

There were other parallels too, in that for naked, ruthless ambition, the Viking era produced rulers to rival Macbeth. A tale from the sagas recounted how the eleventh-century king of Norway Olaf Haraldsson once quizzed three young princes, his half-brothers, about their future hopes. One wished for large estates, a second for cattle by the thousand; but the third said he wanted warriors—enough to eat up all his brother's cows. "That boy will be a king," Olaf commented admiringly. The remark proved prophetic: the stripling was the future Harald Hardrada (see p.124), a battle-hardened ruler of Norway who finally met his death fighting to obtain the English throne at Stamford Bridge in 1066.

THE WARRIOR VISAGE

Norse legend equated the warrior class with the aristocracy and explained its
origins through a story of the god Heimdall. Out walking in human guise one day,
he stopped at the cottage of a pair of peasants, who let him share their roof and their
bed; the result, nine months later, was a son, sturdy but coarse, who was named
Thrall—"Slave." Heimdall next stopped at a farmer's house, with the same outcome,
only this time the baby was named Karl, or "Freeman." Finally Heimdall came to a
nobleman's house, and once more enjoyed the hospitality not just of his host but also
of his wife; and this time the end-product of his visit was a strapping lad who grew
up skilled in the use of the bow and the spear. His name was Jarl, or "Earl," and his
descendants were fighting men—just the sort of warriors, in fact, who might have
worn this helmet from Vendel in Sweden, dated to the seventh or eighth century CE.

FATE AND GLORY

Viking warriors were brought up in a culture that glorified courage, strength, and loyalty. Children imbibed the message from an early age—these lines were supposedly written by the poet and fighter Egil Skalla-Grimsson at the age of 12: *My mother once told me / She'd buy me a longship / A handsome-oared vessel / To go sailing with Vikings; / To stand at the sternpost / And steer the fine sea-steed / Then head back for harbor / And hew down some foemen.*

A 12th-century carving in Hylestad church in Norway shows the hero Gunnar facing death in a snake pit. Gunnar's fictional death at the hands of the tyrant Atli (modeled on Attila the Hun) paralleled the real-life fate of Ragnar Lodbrok (see p.125), whose demise by snakebite was at least purportedly historical.

A bold and bloodthirsty spirit could lead a man to fame, riches, and the very highest honors. One celebrated example was Harald Sigurdsson, half-brother of a murdered king of Norway, who fled his homeland for the East, where he ended up as commander of the Byzantine emperor's Varangian Guard (see pp.82–3). Having made his fortune and his reputation in foreign service, he returned home to claim the crown his brother had lost, going on to rule so autocratically that he went down in history as Harald Hardrada—Harald the Ruthless.

Even so, such glory had to be bought at a cost. For the Norse warrior, the reverse of the coin of worldly fame was a willingness to confront death fearlessly, even in the face of insurmountable odds. Fighting men were expected to show contempt for the "straw death" of those who died in their beds. To avoid it, the legendary hero Starkad hung all his gold around his neck in his old age with the deliberate intention of attracting the notice of potential assassins. The ploy worked, and he was eventually beheaded by the son of a man he had earlier slain. Even so, his martial spirit lived on, if only briefly; according to one version of the story, his body went on fighting for a time even after his head had been cut off.

A mounted warrior decorates a 7th-century runestone from Mojbro in Sweden. For much of the Viking Age, Norsemen rarely fought on horseback, but by the 11th century Normans and other groups had turned themselves into accomplished cavalrymen.

Another famous tale told of a celebrated warrior named Ragnar Lodbrok. Captured by King Ella of Northumbria while fighting in Britain, he was cast into a pit of adders. Far from showing fear, he sang a famous death song: *Gladly shall I drink ale / On high with the Aesir. / My life-days are ended. / I laugh as I die.* Just as memorable was the revenge taken by his sons when they in turn captured King Ella. They killed him by "carving the blood eagle": breaking his ribs and ripping his lungs from his back, where they continued to expand and contract in a motion that mimicked the flapping of the great bird's wings. The Vikings were not squeamish, and cruelty as well as courage was among their hallmarks.

THE ART OF WARFARE

The Vikings' taste for ostentatious ornament extended to their weaponry. Noble
warriors would advertise their status through swords with hilts of gold or silver
rather than the horn that common weapons employed. Ax heads might be
decorated with silver inlay in serpentine designs, while riders embellished their
horses' bridles with lavish metal mounts like the one shown above. Yet the most
spectacular of all a Norse army's accouterments were undoubtedly its shields. Up to
a yard in diameter, they were designed to protect the bearer from chin to knee. For
much of the Viking Age they were circular in form, although kite shapes became
popular in later years, as the Bayeux tapestry shows. They had central bosses of
metal that were sometimes elaborately patterned, but the bulk of the body was
made of wood. Brilliantly painted in reds, yellows, and other primary colors
or in bold abstract patterns, they must have presented a magnificent panoply when
raised in the line of battle or stowed for storage along a longship's gunwales.

THE VIKING ARMORY

Every freeborn Norse male was expected to own weapons, and most knew how to put them to good use. The finest and most costly were the longswords: double-edged blades designed for hacking rather than thrusting and made with a groove known as a fuller along the center of the blade. Swords were treasured possessions that were sometimes given pet names like "Leg-biter" or "Golden-hilt," and were often passed down from father to son. The best were made in the Frankish lands, employing a "pattern-welding" technique that involved combining strips of iron of different hardness for increased suppleness and flexibility.

Next in status among Viking weaponry were the spear and the javelin, used respectively for thrusting and throwing. These were fearsome implements with blades up to a half yard long, attached to ash shafts four or five times that length. In myth they were particularly associated with Odin, who was known as "Lord of the Spear" and whose own weapon, Gungnir, never failed to hit its target. In time the weapons also became linked with the memory of Olaf Tryggvason, king of Norway, a formidable warrior who was said to be able to hurl two spears at once, one from each hand.

Legend likes to portray the Viking raider with battleax in hand, but in fact axes were for the most part relatively humble arms chiefly used by those who could not afford swords. A few richly decorated examples have been found in high-status graves, but for the most part surviving axes are indistinguishable from the tools used by woodsmen to cut down trees; presumably they served both purposes. Like axes, short stabbing knives were also used in battle, as were bows and arrows, although these seem more often to have been employed in hunting; they were particularly linked to the little-known god Ull, perhaps a patron of the hunt.

RIGHT Swords were the Viking weapon par excellence. They were wielded with one hand, leaving the other free to grasp a shield. Some had ornately decorated hilts, a sign of status indicating the wealth of the owner.

LEFT This elaborate helmet, forged in iron and embellished with bronze, was found in one of the 7th-century noblemen's graves at Vendel in Sweden. Most warriors in the Viking era proper made do with conical leather caps.

SHIPS OF STONE

Viking men and women were famously buried in ships, but a parallel tradition, dating back in some areas to the Bronze Age, saw the deceased laid to rest in normal graves that were then marked by standing stones erected in the shape of a boat. The best-known examples are at Lindholm Høje, near Ålborg in northern Jutland, where a Viking Age cemetery that had been covered with sand sometime around the year 1000 was excavated in the 1950s. Not all the 700 or so graves were boat-shaped—there were also squares, circles, and rectangles—but the characteristic longship pattern seems to have become the most popular from about the year 800 on. Most of the bodies at the site were cremated, and so could not have been imagined to be physically traveling after death. Even so, the symbolism seems clear: the soul was embarking on a journey, and for Vikings the usual means of transport over long distances was a boat.

THE FEASTING HALL OF THE DEAD

The Norse peoples had conflicting views about what happened after death. Separate regions, communities, and perhaps even individuals held different ideas about the afterlife and what it held in store.

The best-known of all their beliefs concerned Valhalla, the feasting hall in Asgard where Odin played host to dead kings and warriors. Vikings who gave up their lives on the battlefield were taken there by the Valkyries, battle-maidens whose name meant "Choosers of the Slain." The hall itself was impossibly magnificent: it was said to have 540 doors, each of them wide enough to allow the passage of 800 warriors walking abreast. Its walls were made of glittering spears, its roof of precious shields that bathed it in a golden glow. There the chosen feasted on limitless supplies of mead and on the flesh of the boar Saehrimnir, which was magically made whole again each night.

The warriors still had a part to play in the cosmic scheme, for they made up the ranks of the Einherjar, the army of human heroes who would fight alongside the gods in the final showdown of Ragnarok (see pp.62–5). In the meantime they were expected to keep in training by spending their days fighting one another. However, each evening their wounds instantly healed, permitting them to carouse late into the night to the sound of lutes and pipes and the tales of poets recounting brave deeds of long ago.

There are suggestions that Valhalla was a relatively late addition to the body of Norse myth, and the whole concept has something of a literary ring to it. There is also

Among the most famous of all the Gotland monuments, this stone could stand as a general epitaph for the Viking fighting man. Below, a longship carries sword-bearing warriors to battle; above, the war god Odin, mounted on Sleipnir, and a Valkyrie with a cup of mead wait to welcome to Valhalla those who will die in the field.

a degree of confusion in the myths themselves; some indicate contradictorily that certain dead warriors went instead to Freyja's hall of Folkvanger. Yet the Byzantine historian Leo the Deacon reported that, rather than surrender, Rus warriors would take their own lives in battle, offering themselves up as sacrifices to Odin. This evidence, together with depictions of what could be Valkyries holding out drinking horns to welcome dead warriors on at least a dozen of the Gotland picture-stones, suggests that the notion of Valhalla did indeed have a real place in the Norse cult of the dead.

The fate of those who died the "straw death" at home in bed was far less attractive. They were condemned to a grim afterlife in the shadowy realm of Hel (a word that was borrowed by the

Anglo-Saxons and is the origin of "hell"). This underworld region was ruled by the sinister goddess of the same name, whose body was half living flesh and half rotting cadaver. From Hel they might pass on to the freezing cold of Niflheim, or else be banished to Nastrond, the strand of corpses, where they waded in icy streams of poison before being cast into the cauldron Hvergelmir to feed the monstrous Nidhogg. Such notions may have been affected by Christian ideas of the fate of the wicked.

Alongside the stories told in the myths there went folk traditions and burial customs that apparently told a different story about people's final fate. Loved ones

Mead and ale were often passed around at feasts in drinking horns. Most such vessels came from cattle, but more elaborate artifacts were also put into service. These examples are replicas of two celebrated 5th- or 6th-century golden horns from Gallehus in Denmark, the originals both now lost. (There is no evidence of metal horns anywhere within the strict definition of the Viking period.)

were sometimes laid to rest close to the places where they had lived in the hope that they would linger there after death, continuing to exert a benign influence as in life. In contrast, evil people were buried as far away from habitations as possible for fear that they might rise again as the walking dead, murderous ghouls capable of doing terrible harm to the living. In addition, there even seem to have been Viking Age skeptics who doubted the existence of any life after death. The *Hávamál*, in its earthy wisdom, noted fatalistically: "Wealth dies, kinsmen die, a man himself must likewise die: but fame never dies, for him who achieves it well."

However, to judge from the evidence of burials such views must have been limited to a minority of the population. Excavated graves show that individuals were regularly buried with objects they had used in daily life—warriors with their weapons, women with jewelry and household utensils—presumably in the expectation that they would need them after death. In addition, the prevalence of boat burials—or, in Iceland where people normally rode, of interments incorporating the bones of horses—suggests strongly that people conceived of the passage of the soul as a journey.

One such was described in the myths, when Hermod rode down to Hel in an attempt to ransom the newly dead Baldur from its icy queen. It was a long and bitter voyage of nine nights, through dark valleys leading to the far and frozen North. At its end Odin's messenger had to cross the Gjoll torrent, spanned by a golden-roofed bridge, where Hel's guardian Modgud quizzed him. Then Hermod rode on further north still to Hel gate, which he cleared at a single leap, for he was mounted on the wonderful eight-legged steed Sleipnir. Yet at journey's end all that awaited him was the dark and chill of Hel itself—cold comfort for Hermod and, by implication, for Norse men and women contemplating their own final destiny.

LEFT The northern peoples imagined death as a journey, usually by boat as most long-distance voyages at the time were made over water. The maritime motif recurs not just in ship burials but also in the frequent depiction of longships on memorial stones.

RIGHT Dated to about 900 CE, this silver pendant depicting a woman holding up a drinking horn probably represents a Valkyrie. These mythical battle-maidens had the task of taking newly dead warriors to Valhalla to join the Einherjar—the band of human heroes destined to fight alongside Odin at the final battle of Ragnarok.

VIKING RULERS

KINGS OF NORWAY		KINGS OF DENMARK (THE JELLING DYNASTY)		PRINCES OF KIEVAN RUSSIA		DUKES OF NORMANDY	
ca. 880–930	Harald Fairhair			ca. 862–879	Rurik	911–ca. 925	Rollo (Rolf)
ca. 930–936	Eirik Bloodax	ca. 940–958	Gorm the Old	ca. 879–913	Oleg	ca. 925–942	William Longsword
ca. 936–960	Hakon the Good	958–987	Harald Bluetooth	913–945	Igor	942–996	Richard I
ca. 960–970	Harald Greycloak	987–1014	Svein Forkbeard	945–972	Svyatoslav I	996–1026	Richard II
. . . . . .		1014–1018	Harald II	972–980	Yaropolk I	1026–1027	Richard III
995–1000	Olaf Tryggvason	1019–1035	Knut the Great (King of England 1016–1035)	980–1015	Vladimir	1027–1035	Robert the Magnificent
. . . . . .				1015–1054	Yaroslav the Wise	1035–1087	William the Conqueror (King of England 1066–1087)
1015–1030	Olaf Haraldsson (St.Olaf)	1035–1042	Harthacnut				
1030–1035	Svein Alfivason	1042–1046	Magnus the Good				
1035–1046	Magnus the Good						
1046–1066	Harald Hardrada						

THE NORSE GODS

The Aesir

ODIN

Chief of the Norse gods. God of poetry, having used trickery to steal the Mead of Inspiration from the giant Suttung, who was guarding it. The *Hávamál* recounts that he hung on the World Tree for nine days and nine nights to obtain the secret of runes; perhaps because of this experience, he was known as "The Hanged" and "Lord of the Gallows," and supposedly had the power of bringing hanged men to life. The principal Norse war god, he was associated more with strategy and cunning than with strength or courage; dead warriors went to his hall of Valhalla in Asgard. His prized possessions included the spear Gungnir, which always struck its target, and his eight-legged steed Sleipnir, the finest of horses. Two ravens, Huginn and Muninn, perched on his shoulders, reporting all they had seen and heard. He was one-eyed, having sacrificed the other for a draft from the Well of Knowledge.

THOR

A mighty fighter against the forces of chaos and darkness, Thor was the most popular of the Norse gods and the one to whom people most often appealed for help in times of need. His chief targets were the giants, with whom he frequently fought, and the World Serpent; the two were destined to kill each other at Ragnarok. He wielded the hammer Mjollnir, and he drove about in a chariot pulled by two goats. He was the god of storms, and thunder was thought to be the noise made by his chariot as he rode about the sky. The day-name Thursday derives from his name.

BALDUR

Son of Odin, Baldur was the most beautiful of the Norse gods, and was associated with light and joy. He owes his importance in myth to the events surrounding his death, which was engineered by the jealous Loki; he was eventually killed by a shaft of mistletoe fired unwittingly by his blind twin brother, Hod. Attempts to rescue him from Hel's realm of the dead were again frustrated by Loki. The *Hávamál* recounts that he and Hod shall both eventually be restored to life in the new world that will dawn after the present one has been destroyed at Ragnarok.

LOKI

A trickster god who eventually metamorphoses into a figure of malice and pure evil. Some authorities make him Odin's brother, other merely his blood brother and the son of giants. Loki was closely associated with both Odin and Thor; they shared many adventures and perils, from which they were most often extricated by Loki's cunning. In more sinister vein, he was the father of Hel (the ruler of the underworld), as well as of the wolf Fenrir and Jormungand the World Serpent. Having set in motion the events leading to Ragnarok by engineering the death of Baldur (see above), he was punished by being pinioned on sharp rocks with snakes' venom dropping on his face. He will only be released to lead the forces of evil in the final battle.

HEIMDALL

God of the dawn, Heimdall was the guardian of the rainbow bridge, Bifrost, that joined Midgard to Asgard. He waited there with sword and horn to warn of the approach of the enemies of the gods. On a visit to Midgard, he fathered three children – Thrall (Slave), Karl (Freeman), and Jarl (Earl) – who became the progenitors of the three principal social classes. At Ragnarok, he and Loki are destined to kill one another.

TYR

An early god of war, renowned for his strength and courage. In the later myths he is best remembered for his role in the binding of the wolf Fenrir, which cost him a hand; his final destiny is to die in the course of killing Garm, the hound of Hel, at Ragnarok. His Anglo-Saxon equivalent was Tiw, whose name is commemorated in the day-name Tuesday.

ULL

God of archery and hunting, and also of winter and its allied occupations, including skiing, skating, and snow-shoeing.

IDUNA

The goddess of spring, who kept the golden apples of eternal youth. When these were stolen by the frost giant Thiassi, the gods and the world both started to grow old; the situation was only saved when Loki was prevailed upon to rescue the missing fruit.

FRIGG

Goddess of the clouds and the sky and of housewives and married love. She herself was the wife of Odin and the mother of Baldur and Hod.

The Vanir

NJORD

God of coastal waters and of fishing, and the father of Freyr and Freyja, who accompanied him to Asgard as hostages at the conclusion of the war between the Aesir and the Vanir. In Asgard he married Skadi, the daughter of Thiassi; the couple agreed to divide their lives between his home near the coast and hers high in the mountains, but the arrangement suited neither, and they eventually agreed to live separate lives – a myth generally taken to personify the separation of the northern summer and winter seasons.

FREYJA

The most powerful goddess in the Norse pantheon, mistress of passionate love and fecundity. Famous for her beauty, she was married to Odur and wept tears of gold when he strayed away from her; however, she was not always faithful to him. Her possessions included the Brisingamen necklace and a cloak of feathers that conferred the power of flight. Perhaps, as a patroness of the Valkyries, she also haunted battlefields, and was said to claim half of the dead warriors, who accompanied her back to her hall of Folkvanger. Friday is her name-day.

FREYR

Freyja's twin brother, Freyr was also a fertility god associated with sunshine and rain, prosperity and fruitfulness. His possessions included the golden boar Gullenbursti, which drew his chariot, and a marvellous ship, Skidbladnir, that could travel on land, sea, or air and could be folded up to fit in a pocket when not being used for transportation. He also owned a magical sword, but gave it to his servant Skirnir in return for his help in winning the hand of the earth giantess Gerd, who became his wife. He will thus be left weaponless for the final battle of Ragnarok. Freyr was particularly worshiped at the time of the winter solstice, when people sacrificed for good crops in the coming year; the custom of serving a boar's head at Christmas, which survived into modern times, is said to have been a relic of his cult.

FURTHER READING

Almgren, Bertil., et al. *The Viking*. Nordbok: Gothenburg, Sweden, 1975.

Anon. *Beowulf*, translated by David Wright. Penguin: London,1957.

Crossley-Holland, Kevin. *The Penguin Book of Norse Myths*. Penguin: London, 1980.

Davidson, Hilda Ellis. *Gods and Myths of Northern Europe*. Penguin: London, 1964.

Davidson, Hilda Ellis. *Pagan Scandinavia*. Hamlyn: London, 1984.

Davidson, Hilda Ellis. *The Lost Beliefs of Northern Europe*. Routledge: London, 1993.

Foote, Peter G., and Wilson, David M. *The Viking Achievement*. Praeger: New York, 1970.

Graham-Campbell, James. (ed.) *The Viking World*. Frances Lincoln: London, 1980.

Graham-Campbell, James. (ed.) *Cultural Atlas of the Viking World*. Time-Life Books: Amsterdam, 1994.

Haywood, John. *The Penguin Historical Atlas of the Vikings*. Penguin: London, 1995.

Jones, Gwyn. *A History of the Vikings*. Oxford University Press: Oxford, 1984 (revised ed).

Logan, F. Donald. *The Vikings in History*. Routledge: London & New York, 1991.

Magnusson, Magnus. *Viking: Hammer of the North*. Orbis: London, 1976.

Magnusson, Magnus. *Vikings!* BBC Books: London, 1980.

Magnusson, Magnus. *The Vikings*. Tempus: Stroud, England, 2000 (revised ed).

Page, R.I. *Norse Myths*. British Museum Press: London, 1993.

Roesdahl, Else. *The Vikings*. Penguin: London, 1998 (revised ed).

Sawyer, Peter. *The Age of the Vikings*. Edward Arnold: London, 1960.

Sawyer, Peter. (ed.) *The Oxford Illustrated History of the Vikings*. Oxford University Press: Oxford, 1997.

Simek, R. *Dictionary of Northern Mythology*. Boydell and Brewer: Woodbridge, England, 1993.

Sturluson, Snorri. *The Prose Edda*, translated by Arthur Gilchrist Brodeur. The American-Scandinavian Foundation: New York, 1916.

Taylor, Paul B., and Auden, W.H. *The Elder Edda: A Selection*. Faber & Faber: London, 1969.

Turville-Petre, E.O.G. *Myth and Religion of the North*. Weidenfeld & Nicolson: London, 1964.

Wernick, Robert. *The Vikings*. Time-Life Books: Amsterdam, 1979.

Wilson, David M. *The Northern World*. Harry N. Abrams: New York, 1980.

INDEX

PICTURE CREDITS